EVEREST-ASPIRATION

THE WORKS OF SRI CHINMOY

EVEREST-ASPIRATION

★

LYON · OXFORD

GANAPATI PRESS

LXXXVII

ISBN 978-1-911319-13-9

FIRST EDITION WENT TO PRESS ON 13 AUGUST 2017

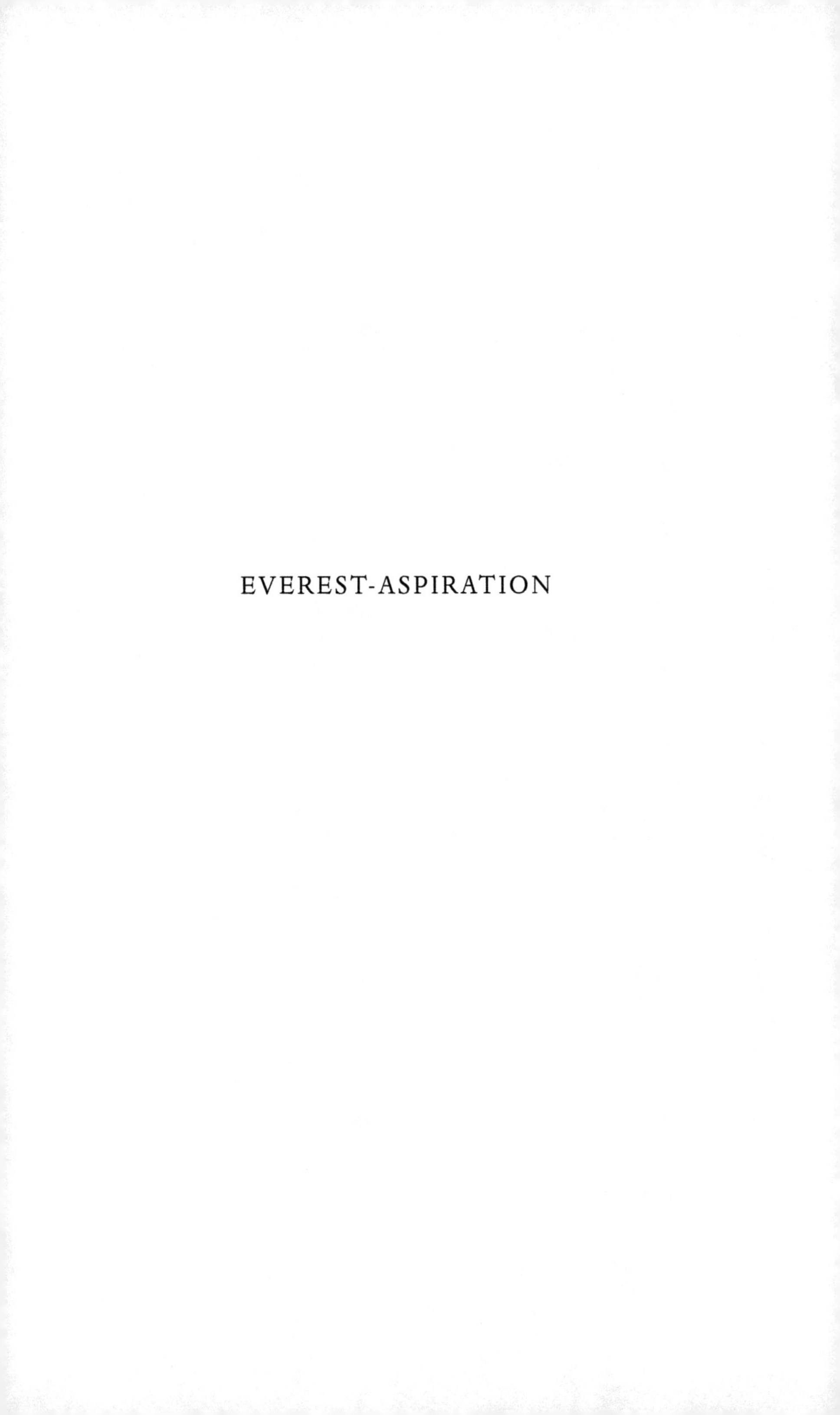

EVEREST-ASPIRATION

EVEREST-ASPIRATION

1. I PRAY, I MEDITATE

I pray to God and meditate on God.

I pray to God because God is my Lord, my Sovereign Lord, my Lord Supreme.

I meditate on God because God is my Friend, my eternal Friend, my only Friend.

I pray to God because He is powerful and thoughtful.

I meditate on God because He is beautiful and fruitful.

I pray to God to see His Face of Height.

I meditate on God to feel His Heart of Delight.

I pray to God to grant me what He is.

I meditate on God to regain what I have lost.

I pray to God to show me the way.

I meditate on God to transform my life of ignorance-night into a life of wisdom-light.

I pray to God to become the sound-sky in my human life.

I meditate on God to become the silence-sun in my divine life.

In my desire-life I pray to God because I am my necessity's slave.

In my aspiration-life I meditate on God because God and I have become our necessity's mutual satisfaction.

My prayer breathlessly loves God's Compassion-Power.

My meditation unconditionally loves God's Justice-Light.

Salvation-gift I have received from my prayer.

Perfection-gift I have received from my meditation.

I pray to God and meditate on God.

EA 1. *1 July 1977, 9:30 p.m. — Woodrow Wilson Hall, Monmouth College, Asbury Park, New Jersey.*

2. GRATITUDE

Gratitude, gratitude, gratitude.

Gratitude is a miracle-action in us. This miracle-action strengthens our physical body, purifies our vital energy, widens our mental vision and intensifies our psychic delight.

The seeker in us tries to be simple, pure, humble, sincere. Every spiritual seeker tries to cultivate these qualities in abundant measure. The easiest and most effective way to cultivate these qualities is to open the gratitude-flower and let it blossom inside our heart petal by petal. How can we do this? Not only do we have to give more importance to what we have, but we also must give all importance to what we do not have.

What we have is wishful thinking, wishful seeking, wishful becoming. Wishful thinking: We think that we shall be great or successful in some way. Wishful seeking: We seek the truth and light in our own way, in the place where we think truth and light must abide. Wishful becoming: This is the most deplorable mistake we make. We want to become something that pleases us. If we want to please ourselves in our own way, then consciously or unconsciously we bring the vital-wolf to the fore.

What we do not have is the breathless inner cry and the measureless outer smile. If we can develop the breathless inner cry, then automatically we develop the measureless outer smile.

Either from within we come without, or from without we dive deep within. We can start our journey either from the soul's capacity or from the body's capacity. Ultimately these two capacities have to be united. Needless to say, the soul's capacity is infinitely greater than the body's capacity. But the little capacity that the body has, has to be united with the soul's capacity. The body's greatest capacity is the acceptance of the soul's leadership. If the soul is accepted as the supreme leader, if the soul gets the opportunity to guide, mould and shape our destiny, then we get what we do not have right now: the sweet, pure, breathless, intense inner cry and the sure, measureless outer smile.

EA 2. 2 *July 1977, 5:30 a.m. — Sri Chinmoy Centre, Jamaica, New York.*

3. I DO NOT KNOW

"I do not know." This is indeed an answer. This answer satisfies the sincere seeker in us, for the sincere seeker does not stoop to insincerity. But we have to know how far this answer can lead us. Can it lead us to our destined Goal? No, never! We have to be able to say, "I know."

In order to find the answer, first we look around us. But the outside world laughs at us, ridicules us and sometimes looks down upon us. It considers us to be the worst possible fools. Then we dive deep within in order to get the answer. At that time something deep within tells us that what we think of ourselves is what we truly are. What we feel ourselves to be is what we truly are. What we shall ultimately become consciously is what we truly are.

What do we think we are? We think that we are devoted instruments and thoughtful seekers. What do we feel ourselves to be? We feel ourselves to be soulful lovers. And what shall we ultimately become? We shall become fruitful servers. Devoted instruments, thoughtful seekers, soulful lovers and fruitful servers of the Supreme: If we can think of ourselves in this way, if we can feel that we are all these things, then there can be no other answer for us either here on earth or there in Heaven.

This is the answer: we are the devoted instruments, the thoughtful seekers, the soulful lovers and the fruitful servers of the Supreme. "I do not know" is now transformed into "I do know." What do I know? I know that I have all along been seeking for the birthless Vision and the ever-transcending Reality of my experience-realisation, my realisation-revelation and my revelation-manifestation.

EA 3. *2 July 1977, 8:30 a.m. — Jamaica High School Track, Jamaica, New York.*

4. DREAM

What is dream? Dream is creation. Creation is either division or union. "Division" is a complicated word. When we use division to divide the existence-reality, we enter into the world of ego and "I"-ness. But again, when we use it to divide work, labour, capacities, at that time it is a veritable blessing. If we divide and, through our division, get the result in a solid, concrete way to form one truth and one reality, then that division is good. But when we divide the reality into pieces and give supremacy to one piece and do not appreciate or value the other pieces, then we sing the song of separativity. This kind of division ends in destruction, the destruction of the little world that we claim to be ours.

"Union" is also a complicated word. When we work together, it is a great blessing. When we mix together, it is a great blessing. But when it is the union of darkness and light, when it is the union of desire and aspiration, then it is a deplorable mistake. The aspiration-life must not mix with the desire-life. If it is to mix, always it must mix with the renunciation-life — the renunciation of unnecessary possessions, of the things that are not divine, illumining and perfect.

With the aspiration-life we have to start our journey. But then there comes a time when we feel that our aspiration-life has blossomed considerably, and is ready to enter into the desire-life to transform it. The aspiration-life has to play the role of the bridge between the desire-life and the realisation-life. The seeker's aspiration-life will enter into the desire-life for the immediate and total transformation of the desire-life. The seeker's realisation-life will enter into the aspiration-life for the perfection of the aspiration-life and for the manifestation of the Absolute Supreme.

Each dream is a creation. Each creation is either conscious aspiration or unconscious aspiration. Our aspiration enters into the desire-life, the little brother, and helps him clean his body, purify his mind and illumine his earthly existence. Each iota of aspiration also expedites the arrival of realisation. Our aspiration enters into the realisation-life or brings the realisation-life into the aspiration-life in order to make the aspiration-life completely perfect for the awakening of our physical reality, and for the blossoming of the soul-reality, which is within us and for us.

A dream is God's creation in the inner world. From the inner world we enter into the realisation-world. Creation and dream, aspiration and realisation — they are all members of the same family. If we can become aware of one, then automatically we can have the other three; for our dream is, after all, a disguised reality, and a disguised reality does not remain always in disguise. It purifies our mind. It offers dynamism to our vital and it offers an inner awakening in our physical reality.

I bow to dream because it is sweet and pure. I bow to reality because it not only has possibility and potentiality but it also has inevitability in boundless measure. I bow to aspiration, for it has love for us inside its boundless existence. But I love realisation, for realisation is the only thing that I need to make my Inner Pilot constantly and supremely happy.

EA 4. *2 July 1977, 3:50 p.m. — Bethpage State Park, Long Island, New York.*

5. SECURITY

Security is life. Insecurity is death. When one is secure in one's life, one sees an hour inside a second. When one is insecure in one's life, one does not see even a second inside an hour.

Secure people smile, not because they have something but because they are something. Secure people belong to an ever-transcending creative force. Insecure people unconsciously and deplorably have made friends with self-doubt, which is the worst possible poison. Once they have made friends with self-doubt, they are forced to make friends with somebody else, and that somebody else is self-destruction.

When one is secure, one guards what one has and what one is. What one has is simplicity, sincerity, serenity, purity and many more divine qualities. These divine qualities have to be guarded. When one is secure, only then is one in a position to guard them. When they are well protected, they can play their respective roles most satisfactorily inside the physical consciousness, vital consciousness and mental consciousness.

Security is an honour that one gives and one gets. When one becomes a security guard, one serves a superior.

The superior is being honoured because he is being guarded by others. The security guard shows the utmost respect, love and adoration to the superior; therefore, the world may think that only the superior is being honoured. But I wish to say that it is a mutual honour.

This is a public park, and undivine people are all around. I am sitting here, and you are around me with folded hands. With your aspiration and devotion you are guarding me from the wrong forces. You are guarding me; therefore, you are honouring me. You are honouring me, true, but I am also honouring you. Out of 140 people I have requested you to come here.

It is the same thing when we pray to God. We think that we are honouring Him. We are honouring him, true, but God has already honoured us by choosing us to be His Instruments. We are honouring Him with our aspiration and devotion. But by His acceptance of us, God is also honouring us. When we serve Him, love Him and cry to Him, at that time we honour Him. But it is He who has given us the opportunity to serve Him and aspire for Him. So the security guard, when he helps or protects the superior in any way, is not at all inferior. He is only honouring and being honoured.

God has given us the capacity, the aspiration, to pray to Him and meditate on Him. By praying and meditating we are honouring Him. Again, using us as His chosen instruments, He is honouring us. When we give our security to Him, we get back His Security. By honouring God through prayer and meditation, we also honour ourselves.

God is secure in us because He dreams in and through us. He is the eternal Life-Tree; we are His projecting branches. We are not aware of our own reality; we are not aware that we are part and parcel of the Life-Tree which is God; therefore, we are insecure. But by praying and meditating we come to realise that the branches, leaves and flowers are part and parcel of the Tree itself. When we realise this, we become secure in the Source and secure in the flow. When the flow realises its absolute Source, it becomes secure. The Source is always secure in the flow, for the Source knows that its own capacity is always boundless.

EA 5. *2 July 1977, 4:38 p.m. — Bethpage State Park, Long Island, New York.*

6. THEORETICAL SURRENDER AND PRACTICAL SURRENDER

Aspiration, my aspiration, long, long ago you told me that the animal life is no good, that it is all destruction. I believed you; therefore, I gave up the animal life. Then you told me that the human life is no good, that it is all bondage. I believed you; therefore, I gave up the human life. Then you told me that there is something infinitely higher than the divine life, and that life is the life of perfect oneness with my Beloved Supreme. I believed you; therefore, I became one with my Beloved Supreme.

Now I am one with my Beloved Supreme and I shall forever remain one, inseparably one, unconditionally one, with my Beloved Supreme. And now you tell me, my aspiration, that just remaining inside my Beloved Supreme and being inseparably one with Him is not enough. I have to be a practical exponent of the Supreme; I have to reveal and manifest what my Beloved Supreme has and is. Theoretical oneness is of no avail. It is the practical oneness with Him that counts. This practical oneness is the constant cheerful execution of His Will.

My theoretical surrendered oneness says:
"Lord, let Thy Will be done." But as soon as I am buffeted by the blows of earthly life, I withdraw my so-called surrendered oneness with my Beloved Supreme. I curse myself for having been eager to become one with Him. This is theoretical surrendered oneness.

My practical surrendered oneness is totally different. In my practical oneness I experience what He experiences in and through me: life's failure and life's success, life's sorrow and life's joy, life in the process of recoiling and withdrawing and life in the process of becoming and transcending. All I accept with cheerful, devoted, unconditional and surrendered oneness. On the physical plane, the practical plane, if I can establish my surrendered oneness with my Beloved Supreme, then only do I become not only what He has but also what He is. What He is, I eternally and truly am: Eternity's Oneness-Soul and Infinity's Oneness-Goal.

My sweet children, a few of you have made a theoretical surrender. But practical surrender nobody, nobody, nobody has made. And there are many here who have not made even the theoretical surrender. So where do I stand with you? Those who have not made the theoretical surrender, kindly from today make this theoretical surrender. And those who have made the theoretical surrender, please try from today to become at every moment a practically surrendered disciple of the Supreme. Those who are now theoretical please try to become practical, and those who have not made even the theoretical surrender please make it a point to come to the level of theoretical oneness with the Supreme.

EA 6. *3 July 1977, 8:37 a.m. — Jamaica High School Track, Jamaica, New York.*

7. SATISFACTION

Each human life is a song. A seeker sings a new song every day. He sings and he discovers. What does he discover? He discovers a body full of enthusiasm, a vital full of determination, a mind full of peace, a heart full of bliss and, finally, a life full of satisfaction.

Satisfaction is needed in the animal life, the human life and the divine life. But the satisfaction that we get in the animal life is not true satisfaction. In the human life also we do not get true satisfaction. Only in the divine life do we get true satisfaction.

In the animal life we try to get satisfaction through destruction. In the human life we try to acquire satisfaction through possession. In the divine life we try to receive satisfaction from illumination. Through destruction the satisfaction that we get is not and cannot be the real satisfaction. Through possession the satisfaction that we get is not and cannot be the real satisfaction. Through illumination the satisfaction that we get is undoubtedly the true satisfaction.

We are all seekers here; we pray and meditate. Inside our prayer, inside our meditation, we always try to see the face of satisfaction. When we pray, we try to go up and achieve satisfaction. When we meditate, we try to bring Light and Delight to the fore from within ourselves, and enjoy satisfaction here inside our body, vital, mind and heart. When we pray, we try and cry to receive something from Above so that our thirst can be quenched. When we meditate, we invoke our own higher realities to manifest in and through us.

Meditation is preceded by concentration and followed by contemplation. Concentration, meditation and contemplation go together. Concentration is the speed, meditation is the confidence and contemplation is the victory. We can safely say that concentration has and is the deer-speed, meditation has and is the elephant-confidence and contemplation has and is the lion-victory.

It is always advisable for us to have speed, for we have to value the goal. The goal is not stationary. Today's goal will be tomorrow's starting point. We are in the process of going towards an ever-transcending, ever-illumining and ever-fulfilling goal, so we have to pay all attention to our speed, to how fast we can go.

Confidence is also of paramount importance. If we have confidence in ourselves and confidence in God, then definitely we can make fast progress. If we have confidence only in God and not in ourselves, we will not be able to go very fast. If we have confidence only in ourselves and not in God, then we will not be able to make any progress, either. We have to feel our confidence in God and God's confidence in us. Our confidence in God we shall feel on the strength of our own dedication, and God's confidence in us we can feel in and through the Compassion-Light which He bestows upon us constantly and unconditionally.

Like us, the soul also deals with life. In the case of the soul, there is the universal life and the transcendental Life. When the soul-bird comes down into the world-arena, it spreads its wings and becomes inseparably one with the universal life. At the end of its earthly sojourn, when the soul returns to its own region, it enters into the transcendental Life. Life is nothing short of God's Dream, and this Dream is birthless and deathless. This birthless and deathless Dream God fulfils in and through His all-embracing and all-fulfilling reality: man.

EA 7. *3 July 1977, 8:35 p.m. — P.S. 86, Jamaica, New York.*

8. COMPASSION-HEIGHT AND JUSTICE-LIGHT

"My Lord Supreme, You are at once Compassion-Height and Justice-Light. Do tell me which of the two You consider to be better."

"My son, if you are brave, then Justice-Light is infinitely better. If you are weak, then Compassion-Height is infinitely better. But I wish to tell you that in the long run both Compassion-Height and Justice-Light reach the same destination. They both fulfil the same purpose.

"In the Cosmic Game sometimes it is obligatory for Me to use Justice-Light. Otherwise, if I use always Compassion-Height, then the progress of the seeker in you will be delayed indefinitely. If the seeker in you can brave Justice-Light, then you are bound to make the fastest progress. But this Justice-Light has to be taken cheerfully, devotedly and soulfully; then only will it serve its purpose. If Justice-Light is taken with reluctance, with fear or just out of necessity's demand, and if there is an inner resistance and rebellious attitude, then Justice-Light will fail in its purpose.

"When I show Justice-Light, My son, you have to feel that it is My Concern in disguise; My Concern for your perfection is coming to the fore. When I show Compassion-Height, it is undoubtedly a slower process. But again, if the seeker in you does not forgive you, although I have forgiven you, if you feel remorse and resolve with your adamantine will not to commit the same mistake, then with My Compassion-Height you can also run the fastest. You can run the fastest by becoming infinitely more conscious and aware and by becoming brutally sincere with yourself and fully charged with divine determination.

"Compassion-Height I use more than Justice-Light, My son, because I know each individual human being on earth is weak. Therefore, I take the slow process. If Justice-Light I could use all the time, then progress would be the fastest. But there is a risk here. The vessel may give way; therefore, I am reluctant to use My Justice-Light as often as I use My Compassion-Height. But when I use Compassion-Height, make it a point to be extremely strict, mercilessly strict, with yourself. It is you who have to be strict with your life so that you can be a better, more illumining, more fulfilling instrument of Mine.

"When I use Justice-Light, take it cheerfully, devotedly and soulfully. When I use Compassion-Height, take it with your gratitude-sea and gratitude-sky and, at the same time, dive deep within and become infinitely more strict with yourself than you have already been. Then there is no blunder that you can commit. Justice-Light and Compassion-Height are one, inseparably one. But according to necessity's demands, My son, I use either Justice-Light or Compassion-Height.

"You, as a divine seeker, a genuine seeker, an unconditional seeker, must remain always happy, whether I use Compassion-Height or Justice-Light with you. If it is Justice-Light, use your happiness in a very constructive way; and if it is Compassion-Height, dive deep within and bring to the fore your gratitude-heart. Then charge your body, vital, mind and heart with adamantine will so that you do not repeat the same deplorable mistake.

"Compassion-Height is the shower, the blessing-shower from Above; it is a torrential rain. Justice-Light is the brilliant sunlight, the scorching heat. Both we need equally in order to collect the bumper crop of realisation from the aspiration-seed which germinates slowly, steadily and unerringly according to the Will of My inner Vision and outer Reality."

EA 8. *4 July 1977, 8:05 a.m. — Jamaica High School Track, Jamaica, New York.*

9. MY DESIRE

Desire, my desire, my lifelong friend, I always stay with you. Since I call you my friend, my lifelong friend, may I ask you for a favour? It is a simple request. I am sure you can grant it if you want to. This is my soulful and breathless request: Three times a day will you just allow me to remain all by myself? Each time I will need only three seconds. That means only nine seconds during the entire day I wish to be alone, without you.

Early in the morning at five o'clock I wish to utter a soulful message to my Beloved Supreme for three seconds. This message is: "O my Beloved Supreme, I love You and nobody else. I love You and nobody else. I love You and nobody else." At twelve o'clock noon, I wish to utter another soulful message to my Beloved Supreme three times: "O my Beloved Supreme, I need You and nobody else. I need You and nobody else. I need You and nobody else." At seven o'clock, when the evening sets in, I wish to utter my third soulful message to my Beloved Supreme: "O my Beloved Supreme, I belong to You and to nobody else. I belong to You and to nobody else. I belong to You and to nobody else."

Only nine seconds a day I wish to have from you, O my lifelong friend, O my desire. If you grant me this boon, then there shall come a time when I shall, in return, give you something that you never imagined and never deserved. I shall give you what I shall acquire: my heart's boundless joy to feed you, my soul's boundless light to please you and my God's eternal, infinite and immortal Beauty. O my desire-friend, my lifelong friend, I wish only nine seconds a day to be all by myself. If you fulfil my request, I shall give you things that you will otherwise never be able to receive either in this incarnation or in any incarnation. So, my dear desire-friend, just grant my request: three seconds, three seconds, three seconds — nine seconds a day allow me to be with myself, in myself and for myself. For the Real in me and with the Real in me I wish to remain for nine seconds a day.

EA 9. *4 July 1977, 8:05 p.m. — Informal gathering at a disciple's house, Jamaica, New York.*

10. THE SHORT CUT, THE SHORTER CUT, THE SHORTEST CUT

"My sweet Lord Supreme, I am truly tired of this long road. The road that divides us is very long. Please, please grant me a short cut. I shall be eternally grateful to You if You grant me a short cut to reach You."

"My son, I am surprised to hear that you want to have a short cut, for I thought that someday you would ask Me for the shortest cut. You are ready to be satisfied with only a short cut, but I shall give you a short cut, and I shall also tell you the shorter cut and the shortest cut, in case you need them in the near future.

"The short cut is belief; you must believe in Me. You must believe in Me constantly. Just repeat to yourself: 'I believe in God, I believe in God.' This is undoubtedly an excellent short cut.

"The shorter cut is to repeat to yourself: 'My Lord Supreme loves me infinitely more than I love myself. My Lord Supreme loves me infinitely more than I love myself.' How can it be possible? It is possible because when you see your shortcomings in teeming measure, you get frustrated and you want to destroy yourself. But I see you as a projection of My own Reality; therefore, I do not get frustrated. I am ready to go on with infinite Patience, and this Patience is undoubtedly your salvation. So you can see that I do love you infinitely more than you love yourself.

"The shortest cut is this: You have to tell yourself that you need Me breathlessly. In My case, I will tell you that I need you unmistakably. You need Me breathlessly and I need you unmistakably. This has to be your constant, sincere prayer.

"If you can repeat to yourself that you believe in Me, this is the short cut. If you can say that I love you infinitely more than you love yourself, this is the shorter cut. And the shortest cut is to feel that you need Me breathlessly and I need you unmistakably. If you can do all these, then the short, shorter and shortest cuts will be open to you.

"For Me also there is a short cut, a shorter cut and a shortest cut to reach you. The short cut is when I tell Myself that in you I shall discover the most perfect instrument of Mine. The shorter cut is when I tell Myself that I always love you unconditionally, no matter what you do, no matter what you think of Me, no matter what you tell Me, no matter what happens to you, no matter what you want to do with your life's vision and your life's reality. And the shortest cut is when I see in you My Eternity's Soul and keep for you My Infinity's Goal."

EA 10. *5 July 1977, 8:10 a.m. — Jamaica High School Track, Jamaica, New York.*

11. HAPPINESS AND UNHAPPINESS

Happiness and unhappiness. We all know that happiness and unhappiness are two opposite realities. They are diametrically opposite realities. But there are some people who unfortunately feel that unhappiness is the true happiness. What we call happiness, according to them that very thing is unhappiness; and what we call unhappiness, they call happiness. They are never, never satisfied unless and until they are unhappy, frustrated and miserable. When they are in a melancholy state, they feel that this is the true satisfaction.

To us this is the height of absurdity. We look around and see that unhappiness is singing, dancing, flying everywhere. Unhappiness, in a sense, is running riot. But as if this unhappiness were not enough for these people, they want to add more unhappiness to their system. The unhappiness that they already have they do not try to get rid of. Instead, they want to add more unhappiness in order to derive satisfaction.

Sometimes there are minor calamities, accidents and crises in life that make us unhappy. But we should not think that God sends us these calamities in order to make us pure, or to make our progress fast. No. On very rare occasions we see that saintly people, good people, spiritual people, suffer. When they do, they suffer for various reasons. If they are spiritual Masters of a very high calibre, they suffer on the strength of their oneness with their disciples, their followers, their intimate ones. Again, sometimes God wants to show the world at large that even the great seekers and Masters go through suffering, so people will see that suffering is not something uncommon. He wants to show the world that suffering is inherent in human nature. But in no way does God want to punish us so that He can make us close to Him.

Some people go one step farther. They think that if they can suffer severely and then pray to God, at that time God will listen to their prayers; therefore, deliberately they do something wrong. They know the penalty and they are ready to pay the penalty because they feel that when they suffer God will listen to their prayers. But this is absurd. It is like cutting off your legs and then asking yourself to walk. It is impossible. It is like blinding your eyes and then asking yourself to see. It is impossible. In order to please God, no seeker should deliberately welcome suffering, which is the cause of unhappiness or the same thing as unhappiness.

When you are frustrated or disappointed, at that time if you pray, do not think that the Supreme in me or the Supreme in you will be more pleased. Far from it. When you are frustrated, you are only blocking the road between you and God. At that time you have built a solid wall, an adamantine wall, between yourself and me.

Just be happy and keep your heart open to light and bliss. If you are happy and cheerful, then you can run the fastest. Even if you are not happy, when you come to me you have to force yourself to be happy. By forcing yourself to be happy you can create a kind of receptivity for a few seconds. Then I will be in a position to pour my compassion, light and blessings into you. But if you come to me with a sad face, making me feel that you are dead or that you are about to die right now, then inwardly I can only tell you, "Die, then. I will be there to watch you."

Do not come to me with a sad and frustrated face. If you come to me with an unhappy face, you are only digging your own grave. Even if you have been unhappy the whole day, when you come to me keep a cheerful face. Force yourself to smile. If a child does not want to eat and his mother forces him to eat, then he will be nourished; he will get strength. If a naughty boy does not want to wash, when his mother forces him to wash, he becomes clean in spite of himself. The mind and vital are like naughty boys. So wash them, cleanse them with your soul's light, with your heart's inner cry.

So, my children, always come to me with a cheerful face. Then you will be able to receive whatever I want to give. If you feel that by being unhappy you will become closer to me, or if you feel that your unhappiness itself is happiness, then you will be able to receive nothing. Happiness is happiness. Unhappiness is unhappiness. Night is night.

Let us not make fools of ourselves. Always we have to see the truth in its proper aspect. If it is unhappiness, it is unhappiness. If it is happiness, it is happiness. We have to conquer unhappiness through happiness. This is the only way to run the fastest and create immediate and boundless receptivity. This is the only way to please the Supreme in His own Way.

EA 11. *5 July 1977, 9:05 p.m. — Martin Van Buren High School, Hollis, New York.*

12. HUMAN REALITY AND DIVINE REALITY

"My sweet Beloved Supreme, I know that You have two realities, two aspects — a human reality or human aspect and a divine reality or divine aspect. Please tell me which aspect of Yours is the better of the two, or which aspect of Yours I must choose in order to make the fastest progress, or if it is obligatory on my part to choose one of the aspects in order to arrive at the highest Goal deep within You."

"O seeker-son, I wish to tell you that it is supremely necessary for you to approach both aspects of Me, the human and the divine. It is better to start with the human aspect, for in the human aspect you get encouragement and inspiration sooner than in the divine aspect. In the divine aspect sometimes you may see some austerity in Me, some very hard and fast rules, some strict discipline. But in the human aspect you will see that there are quite a few things which you do that I do in the same manner; therefore, you will get tremendous encouragement. You can sing, you can talk, you can play, you can do sports just as I do. Only when it is a matter of meditation, you cannot do it right now the way I do. That is the only place where you are badly lacking. I do infinitely better meditation than you do. But there are quite a few things which you do as well as I do, and sometimes you may even far surpass Me. Because you have the same capacity that I have in so many things, you are bound to feel that you can arrive at the same footing on the spiritual plane as well. So you get encouragement.

"You have to think of the human aspect and the divine aspect as the flower and the fruit of the tree. I am the Life-Tree, and I bear flowers and fruits. A flower is beautiful. It inspires you, and when you are surcharged with inspiration you run, dive and fly. But there is something more than inspiration; it is called hunger. You are inspired to do something, but you need the inner hunger to strengthen you. That inner hunger is aspiration. When you are hungry, only then do you get the fruits and eat them. My Life-Tree holds the divine aspect in the fruit-form. When you eat the fruit, you get nourishment.

"Again, at times you have to take both the human aspect and the divine aspect together. You have to think of Me as the ocean and yourself as a tiny drop or wave. If you want to see Me or play with Me, you have to feel that I am the ocean and you are inside the ocean as a drop or a surge. If you are wise, then you will see that no matter what you are, you have to remain inside the ocean, inside the vast expanse. The surge cannot contain the ocean, the drop cannot contain the ocean, whereas the ocean can contain the drop and the surge. In fact, they are inseparable. The human aspect you embody, and the divine aspect I embody, but they are inseparably one. Now you have taken the form of a tiny drop and I have taken the form of the ocean. But when you grow up in spiritual matters, at that time you will see that sometimes I become the tiny drop or wave, and you become the ocean. In this way we play hide-and-seek with each other.

"If you want to go from the human to the divine aspect, this is very good. You can also go from the divine to the human aspect. Again, you can accept the human and the divine together. The human aspect is sweet, sweeter, sweetest. The divine aspect is intimate, more intimate, most intimate. This is how the seeker approaches the human aspect and the divine aspect. I am your Beloved Lord Supreme, and you are the seeker in Me, for Me."

EA 12. *6 July 1977, 7:50 a.m. — Jamaica High School Track, Jamaica, New York.*

13. I AM GRATEFUL

I am grateful to my Beloved Supreme, for out of His infinite Bounty He has given me the capacity to love Him more than I love myself.

I am grateful to my Beloved Supreme, for out of His infinite Bounty He has given me the capacity to feel His Need more than my own need.

I am grateful to my Beloved Supreme, for out of His infinite Bounty He has given me the capacity not to drag Him into my desire-world, but to implore His Presence in my aspiration-world, and also to offer Him my earth-bound will and desire-life, and soulfully declare, "Let Thy Will be done."

I shall be extremely grateful to my Beloved Supreme the day He makes me a chosen instrument of His.

I shall be extremely, extremely grateful to my Beloved Supreme the day I can feel that my soul-bird lives only for Him inside my body-cage here on earth and there in Heaven.

I shall be extremely, extremely and extremely grateful to my Beloved Supreme the day I can declare to the world within and to the world without that I am what He has and I have what He is.

EA 13. *6 July 1977, 9:20 p.m. — Unitarian Church, Flushing, New York.*

14. AUSTERITY

"My Lord Supreme, I have heard so much from so many people about austerity. Do enlighten me. I wish to hear from You, from Your Lips, what austerity actually means. Is austerity a kind of self-torture, or is austerity a kind of severe self-discipline?"

"O seeker, discipline and austerity are two different things. They are like the North Pole and the South Pole. You discipline yourself so that you do not get attacks from temptation. You discipline yourself so that the world of the immediate future will come to you with its gifts: happiness and peace of mind. These two gifts are of paramount importance. Even while you are disciplining yourself you get tremendous joy, and the after-effect of discipline is also joy and achievement, veritable achievement.

"But austerity is self-torture. You torture yourself, thinking that I will be highly pleased with you. But that notion is absurd. I am all Love. In order to reach Me, what you need is also love.

"Why do you want to go through austerity? You have the body, the vital, the mind and the heart. These are the members of your immediate family, and you are putting up with them. To put up with your lethargic body, to put up with your aggressive vital, to put up with your doubtful mind, to put up with your impure heart — is that not a form of self-torture? If you are so fond of austerity, then you have to know that already you are performing the most difficult type of austerity by having patience with your impossible body, vital, mind and heart. You do not need any further austerities.

"Just go through discipline. From discipline you will get peace of mind, and in peace of mind I have kept everything for you: peace, love, light and delight in abundant measure. If you are fond of austerity, then I wish to say, abstain from ignorance-food. Austerity is not and cannot be the achievement of any seeker. Discipline is and has to be always, always the achievement of the seeker in you and in everyone. Discipline is your constant opening, constant receptivity to a higher light. Through discipline you have to feel that you are invoking a higher light. When you do sports, when you sing, when you do anything, always feel that you are disciplining the physical consciousness, the vital consciousness, the mental consciousness and the psychic consciousness. Through this discipline not only will you eventually arrive at the Perfection-Goal, but you will become the Goal itself.

"Each thought properly regulated, each action properly regulated, is discipline. Inside discipline, all that I have is for you, O seeker, for you. Love, Peace, Light and Delight in measureless measure: all these I have kept for you inside discipline. For you is the path of discipline, never the path of austerity or self-mortification."

EA 14. *7 July 1977, 7:15 a.m. — Jamaica High School Track, Jamaica, New York.*

15. SMILE, LOVE AND CLAIM

Smile, my friends, my soulful friends, smile. Let us smile. True, this world of ours is full of suffering and excruciating pangs, but that is no reason why we should not smile. We must smile in order to unburden the world's suffering-burden. We must smile in order to diminish its untold pangs.

Love, my friends, my soulful friends, love. Let us love. True, this world of ours is full of hatred and disbelief, but that is no reason why we should not love and why we should not believe. We must love and believe in order to empty the hatred-sea. We must love and believe in order to break asunder the cliffs and peaks of disbelief-mountain.

Claim, my friends, my soulful friends, claim. Let us claim. True, this world of ours has deceived us and betrayed us. Nevertheless, we must claim the world, for it is our bounden duty to change the face of the world. Unless and until we claim the world, we can never transform this world; therefore, we must claim this world as our own, very own, with a view to transforming it.

Finally, we must not forget to smile at our Beloved Supreme, to love our Beloved Supreme and to claim our Beloved Supreme, for He is our Eternity's own, and we are His Eternity's own.

We shall smile at our Beloved Supreme precisely because He is divinely great. We shall love our Beloved Supreme precisely because He is supremely good. We shall claim our Beloved Supreme precisely because we are His Eternity's chosen instruments. Him to please in His own Way, Him to fulfil in His own Way — it is for this we all saw the light of day. He is our Source. In Him we see, in Him we feel, in Him we fulfil our journey's course.

Smile, love and claim. This world of ours is undoubtedly a projection of our Beloved Supreme, although it is far from perfection. But there will come a time when we shall be able to radically transform the face of this world and turn it into Perfection-Reality.

Let us smile at God, love Him and claim Him, for He is all-where only for us, unconditionally for us.

EA 15. *7 July 1977, 9:15 p.m. — Caldwell College, Caldwell, New Jersey.*

16. IMAGINATION

Imagination, O imagination! How do I use my imagination?

I use my imagination to forget my past failures.

I use my imagination to brave my present challenges.

I use my imagination to welcome my future dawn.

I use my imagination to touch and feel my Lord's Compassion-Feet.

I use my imagination to drink deep my Lord's Nectar-Heart.

I use my imagination to see my Lord's Vision-Eye.

I use my imagination to touch my Lord's Assurance-Arms.

I use my imagination to become an exact prototype of my Lord's Heaven-Beauty.

I use my imagination to become a co-sharer of my Lord's earth-responsibility.

What is my imagination? My imagination is the harbinger of my aspiration-tree.

What is my aspiration? My aspiration is the builder of my realisation-palace.

What is my realisation? My realisation is my Lord's and my oneness-song.

EA 16. *8 July 1977, 7:35 a.m. — Jamaica High School Track, Jamaica, New York.*

17. MY LIFELONG FRIENDS

Simplicity is my lifelong friend. My simplicity-friend has cut down my desire-tree.

Sincerity is my lifelong friend. My sincerity-friend has snapped my guilt-conscience-chain.

Purity is my lifelong friend. My purity-friend has secretly told me that love is the only force, the illumining force, the fulfilling force, the supreme force.

Divinity is my lifelong friend. My friend divinity teaches me how to live always inside the Source and how to live only for the Source, the perennial Source.

Immortality is my lifelong friend. My friend Immortality tells me that here on earth my heart's inner cry is the only thing immortal, and there in Heaven my soul's smile is the only thing immortal.

My Beloved Supreme is my lifelong Friend. My Friend, my Beloved Supreme, tells me that here on earth His Grace is my only salvation, and there in Heaven His Face is my only satisfaction.

O my simplicity, sincerity, purity, divinity, Immortality and Beloved Supreme friends, to each of you I offer my own Eternity's gratitude-heart, my own Infinity's oneness-source, my own Immortality's perfection-delight.

EA 17. *8 July 1977, 12:35 p.m. — Dag Hammarskjold Auditorium, United Nations, New York.*

18. ASPIRATION

How do I use my aspiration?

I use my aspiration to unite my earth's ascending cry and my Heaven's descending smile.

I use my aspiration to transform my world's desire-night into my world's illumination-height. I use my aspiration to feed my hungry Beloved Supreme; Him I feed with my aspiration's gratitude-flames.

I use my aspiration to unlearn everything that my earth-bound mind has taught me, and right from the beginning to learn everything from my Heaven-free soul.

I use my aspiration to be the most intimate friend of my sweet, kind and beautiful oneness-heart.

I use my aspiration for success in the outer world and for progress in the inner world. When I succeed, the outer world smiles at me, appreciates me, adores me and extols me to the skies. When I progress soulfully, devotedly and unconditionally, my Beloved Supreme smiles at me, blesses me and embraces me.

What is aspiration? Aspiration is my self-giving.

What is self-giving? Self-giving is a supreme art. From this art I come to realise that I have to fathom my unknown realities and I have to know my higher self which abides deep in the inmost recesses of my heart. I have to become consciously and inseparably one with my higher self, which is in perfect tune with my Beloved Supreme constantly, and I have to manifest my yet-unmanifested realities.

My aspiration embodies concentration, meditation and contemplation.

Concentration is my speed. With this speed I run fast, faster and fastest towards my Beloved Supreme.

Meditation is my depth, my silence-depth. With this silence-depth I invoke my sweet Lord Supreme and place Him deep inside my gratitude-heart.

Contemplation is my ecstasy. With this ecstasy I sing my oneness-song with my Eternity's Father Supreme. With my contemplation-ecstasy I dance my satisfaction-dance with my Lord, who is my Eternity's Friend and Companion. With my Lord the Father I sing. With my Lord the Friend I dance.

EA 18. *8 July 1977, 9:30 p.m. — Manhattanville College, Purchase, New York.*

19. REALISATION

How do I use my realisation?

I use my realisation to taste humanity's poverty.

I use my realisation to taste divinity's prosperity.

I use my realisation to love humanity's tears.

I use my realisation to love divinity's smiles.

I use my realisation to give humanity what I have: hope, hope, hope.

I use my realisation to give divinity what I am: promise, promise, promise.

I use my realisation to free and also to bind. I use my realisation to free the finite, to liberate the finite inside the heart-vision of the Infinite. I use my realisation to bind the Infinite inside the manifestation-body-mission of the finite.

What is realisation? Realisation is my sweet remembrance of my forgotten past.

What is realisation? Realisation is my recovery from my ignorance-disease which has troubled me for millennia.

What is realisation? Realisation is my conscious and constant sailing with my Inner Pilot in His Golden Boat towards the uncharted land, where sooner than at once beauty, divinity and Immortality seeds grow into the richest harvest.

EA 19. *9 July 1977, 7:50 a.m. — Jamaica High School Track, Jamaica, New York.*

20. A FLEETING LIFE

A fleeting life is all we have. So why do we boast, why do we disproportionately exaggerate our earthly, mortal and brittle achievements? The physical in us, no matter how strong, fails us when the Prince of Gloom appears. When death appears, the physical deserts us no matter how strong it is, the vital deserts us no matter how enthusiastic it is, the mind deserts us no matter how brilliant it is, the heart deserts us no matter how kind and pure it is.

A fleeting life is all we have. Why then do we listen to the dictates of the physical world, the temptation-world? Why? Why? Why do we not listen to the dictates of the all-illumining and all-fulfilling soul? Why? Why? Why do we dine each night, all night long, with ignorance-sea? Why do we sport with darkness-dragon every day, all day long? Why? Why? Why do we not love God even conditionally, if it is impossible for us to love God unconditionally? Why? Why?

A fleeting life is all we have. Why do we not please God partially, if it is not within our capacity to please God totally and unreservedly? Why? Why? Can we not say to God once and for all that, although we have given all of our previous lives, even to the previous second, to ignorance-night, from now on we shall give this fleeting life of ours to Him alone? Can we not give God the full authority to guide us, mould us and shape us in His own Way? Since we have failed in the hands of ignorance, can we not give God a chance to direct our life? If God too fails, then we shall see what we ourselves can do with our life. But is it not fair on our part at least to give God a chance, as countless times we have given chances to ignorance-night? Let this short incarnation of ours be offered to God and God alone. If we offer our life to God, then ours will be the life short in years but long in achievements.

God says to us, "Children, I have promised you that I shall not misuse you, I shall not misguide you. I shall prove to you that I can make new personalities, new realities and new divinities out of you; only give Me a chance. As you have time and again given chances to ignorance, even so, for this short, fleeting time give Me the chance and see what I can do for you, since you cannot see what I have already done for you.

"Children, give Me a chance and see what I can do in this fleeting life of yours. This fleeting life can be expanded and extended, My children, if you care to envision My Divinity with your surrendered heart and with your oneness-soul. A fleeting life need not and cannot be the last word of the earth-arena. An endless life, a birthless and deathless life, can alone satisfy man, the future God."

EA 20. *9 July 1977, 11:25 a.m. — John F Kennedy High School, Bronx, New York.*

21. I WISH TO BE FREE

I wish to be free from restlessness, fear and doubt. Restlessness slows down my speed, my inner speed. Fear unnerves me. Doubt poisons me. I need quietude to replace my restlessness. I need courage to replace my fear. I need faith to replace my doubt. My quietude is my confidence, my Lord's assurance. My courage shall serve God the man throughout the length and breadth of the world. My courage shall love man the God in the inner world and in the outer world. My faith shall expedite not only my journey, but the journey of all sincere seekers; for we are one, inseparably one. The strength of my faith will strengthen them and the strength of their faith will strengthen me.

I wish to be free from insincerity, insecurity and impurity. Insincerity separates me from my Lord's greatness. Insecurity separates me from my Lord's vastness. Impurity separates me from my Lord's closeness. Sincerity will replace my insincerity. Security will replace my insecurity. Purity will replace my impurity. My sincerity from now on will be my safeguard; it will always save me from inner and outer destruction. My security will make me feel that my Source, my Beloved Supreme, is always for me, for me, for me, for me. No matter what I do or what I say, He is eternally for me. My purity will enable me to speak to Him, sing with Him and sport with Him here, there and all-where at every moment.

I wish to be free from self-imposition, self-exposition and self-exploitation. I shall not impose any more severe, ruthless austerity on my life, for that is not the right way. I shall not expose my ignorance-dream to the world at large any more. I shall not exploit myself any more. I have already exploited my Supreme's Compassion infinite. I have already exploited the world's abundant patience. I have already exploited my weak helplessness. But I shall not exploit God, I shall not exploit the world and I shall not exploit myself any more.

I wish to be free from what I am in the outer world and from what I am in the inner world. Right now in the outer world I am a hopeless hope, and in the inner world I am a fruitless promise. I want to transform my hope-world into a reality-world, the reality which is fulfilment itself. I want to transform my fruitless promise into fruitful action. This I can do only on the strength of my sleepless inner cry. I can cultivate my inner cry only when I offer to my Beloved Supreme the most precious thing that He has granted me out of His infinite Bounty, and this most precious thing is the tiny flame of my gratitude-heart.

EA 21. *9 July 1977, 3:20 p.m. — Norwalk High School, Norwalk, Connecticut.*

22. EXPERIENCE AND REALISATION

Experience prepares; realisation shares. Experience prepares the seeker for God's choice Hour. Realisation shares God with the seeker. Experience tirelessly tries and cries to find the goal. Realisation effortlessly lives in the goal and eventually grows into the goal itself. Experience secretly tells the seeker what he will ultimately become; he will become God's most perfect instrument. Realisation smilingly tells the seeker what he eternally is here on earth and there in Heaven. On earth he is God the aspiring and evolving man. In Heaven he is man the illumining and fulfilling God.

Experience is convinced of the fact that this world of ours is a battlefield. Here, bad and good, divine and undivine forces are constantly at war. Realisation knows that this world of ours is not a battlefield. It spontaneously knows that this world of ours is God's all-transcending Vision-Tree and God's all-nourishing Reality-Fruit.

Experience moves from the finite to the Infinite. It feels its presence in the finite first and then in the Infinite. It feels its sole identity with the finite drop and then with the infinite sea. Realisation swims right from the beginning inside the infinite sea with God the eternal Swimmer.

Each experience is an added strength in the process of our evolving life. While we are marching along Eternity's road, each experience is an added strength. Each realisation is a transcending triumph. While we are running fast, faster, fastest along Eternity's road, each realisation is a transcending triumph.

Experience is exceedingly fond of God the Compassion-Father. Realisation is exceedingly fond of God the Oneness-Lover.

Experience is our journey's birth. Realisation is our ever-transcending, ever-illumining and ever-fulfilling journey itself.

EA 22. *9 July 1977, 9:20 p.m. — North Avenue Presbyterian Church, New Rochelle, New York.*

23. I AM A BORN PRAYER

I am a born prayer. I am extremely grateful to my Beloved Supreme, for He has given me the prayer-capacity to become one with the Christ consciousness.

I am a born concentration. I am extremely grateful to my Beloved Supreme, for He has given me the concentration-capacity to become one with the Brahma consciousness.

I am a born meditation. I am extremely grateful to my Beloved Supreme, for He has given me the meditation-capacity to become one with the Vishnu consciousness.

I am a born contemplation. I am extremely grateful to my Beloved Supreme, for He has given me the contemplation-capacity to become one with the Shiva consciousness.

I am a born aspiration. I am extremely grateful to my Beloved Supreme, for He has given me the aspiration-capacity to become one with the Ramakrishna consciousness.

I am a born dedication. I am extremely grateful to my Beloved Supreme, for He has given me the dedication-capacity to become one with the Buddha consciousness.

I am a born realisation. I am extremely grateful to my Beloved Supreme, for He has given me the realisation-capacity to become one with the Chinmoy consciousness.

I am a born manifestation. I am extremely grateful to my Beloved Supreme, for He has given me the manifestation-capacity to become one with the Shankara and Vivekananda consciousness.

I am a born perfection. I am extremely grateful to my Beloved Supreme, for He has given me the perfection-capacity to become one with the Krishna consciousness.

I am a born satisfaction. I am extremely grateful to my Beloved Supreme, for He has given me the satisfaction-capacity to become one with Him, with His Consciousness that is already manifested and with His Consciousness that is yet to be manifested.

EA 23. *10 July 1977, 8:15 a.m. — Jamaica High School Track, Jamaica, New York.*

24. YOU ARE SPIRITUAL

You are spiritual. That means you have only a few desires, very, very few desires. One day you will come to the point where you will have only one desire: God. God-realisation will be your only desire. Only one desire will be left you, and that desire will be fulfilled by God Himself with the deepest Love, Joy and Pride.

You are spiritual. That means you are sincere. There are two types of sincerity. One is human sincerity, the mind's sincerity. The other is divine sincerity, the heart's sincerity. The human sincerity that you speak of comes from the most developed member of your human family, the mind. The mind tells you that this is sincerity, this is insincerity. The mind inspires or commands you to say the right thing, the sincere thing. But there is also something called the heart's sincerity. The heart's sincerity is a different matter. Heart's sincerity is oneness with the Will of the Supreme. Sometimes the mind is sincere, but only when the mind can get some profit or benefit from sincerity. Sometimes the mind is sincere because it feels an inner compulsion; it feels inwardly obliged. But in the heart's sincerity, which is oneness with the Supreme's Will, there is an inner, special purpose which the human mind cannot fathom. If you are spiritual, you will be ready eventually to unite your will with the Supreme's Will. That kind of sincerity you are aiming at.

You are spiritual. That means you are humble. Here humility means the acceptance of the world's burden according to your capacity. God is all Humility. He has accepted as His own lot the entire weight of the world. So you also accept the burden around you, according to your limited capacity.

You are like a tree. The tree carries leaves, flowers, fruits and everything. You also can bear the burden of the world around you on your head and shoulders. This is your humility.

You are spiritual. That means you are secure. Security means that you feel the living Presence of God inside you, and you feel your living presence inside God. Also, you tell yourself that you are for God and that God is for you. When you tell yourself that God is for you and you are for God, and when you feel your presence inside God and God's Presence inside you, that is your security.

You are spiritual. That means you are pure. What kind of purity are you aiming at? You are aiming at the purity that will satisfy God and capture Him inside your heart, inside your mind, inside your vital and inside your body. All your impurity will leave you when God comes to live inside your body-room, vital-room, mind-room and heart-room. If you can feel that God is living inside you, then only can you develop real purity.

You are spiritual. That means you are divine. At first your divinity will say that there is no adamantine wall between you and God. You are facing God and God is facing you. Your divinity will make you feel that two Gods are facing each other and conversing. But eventually you will merge into the God that you are now facing. You will know there is only one God and that the entire world is His projection. Then there will come a time when God will ask you to play His role. He will make you feel that you are God and He is your projection. Then He will hide Himself and play the role of the universe, while you play the role of God. He becomes the creation and you become the Creator. You are God's creation according to His Vision, Mission and Necessity. But when

He is fully satisfied with your spirituality, He says, "My son, I am changing the game. I shall become the creation and you become the Creator." This is how you become inseparably one with the Source who conceived of you and created you.

EA 24. *11 July 1977, 8:10 a.m. — Jamaica High School Track, Jamaica, New York.*

25. SPIRITUALITY

Spirituality is man's conscious longing for God. Spirituality tells us that God, who is unknowable today, will tomorrow become knowable and, the day after, will become totally known.

We must need God for God's sake. God can fulfil us in our own way, but it is we who will not be truly fulfilled when God satisfies us in our own way. Our crying heart, our aspiring heart, our illumining heart, will never be satisfied unless and until it pleases God in God's own Way; therefore, our God-realisation is for God's sake. Man's perfection lies in God-satisfaction.

A beginningless beginning tells us that spirituality is an aspiration-plant. This plant grows and grows; eternally it grows. An endless end tells us that spirituality is a surrender-tree. This tree bears divine fruits, and these fruits come to us on the strength of our constant, conscious and surrendered oneness with our Beloved Supreme.

True spirituality is our conscious acceptance of life, not the annulment, not the negation, not the annihilation of life. We must needs accept life and radically change the face of life into the very image of our Beloved Supreme.

Spirituality says to the heart, "O heart, why do you remain insecure? Do you not feel that inside you the Almighty, the Lord Supreme, abides? You must not feel insecure, for it is you who can proclaim to the world at large that inside you is the living Presence of the Beloved Supreme. Of all the parts of the being, you have been chosen to be the first and foremost instrument to guide the mind, the vital and the body to the soul. The soul eventually will bring them to me."

Spirituality tells the mind to remain silent. It says to the mind, "O mind, do not think any more. Your thinking power is nothing short of confusion. You confuse the other members of your family — body, vital and heart — and, at the same time, you are yourself confused when you indulge in the thought-world."

Spirituality says to the vital, "O vital, do not crave. Do not crave for name and fame. Do not crave for anything, for even if you possess the things that you crave, these possessions will not satisfy you. Even inside these possessions there will be a cry for more possessions. You will always act like a beggar if you crave for anything. No matter what you get, you will remain dissatisfied and unfulfilled. So do not walk along that path. Your craving must come to an end. Do not crave anything."

Finally, spirituality says to the body, "O body, how long will you sleep? Don't you know that you have been sleeping from time immemorial? It is because of your ignorance-sleep that the rest of the members of your family are not able to reach the Golden Shore, the destined Goal. O body, sleep not! The Goal is only for those who are awakened. Awake, arise! The rest of the members of your family will run faster than the fastest the moment you become active and dynamic and cast aside the shackles of ignorance-sleep."

Spirituality tells the seeker not to live in the hoary past, not to live in the remote future, but to live in the immediacy of today, in the eternal Now. This eternal Now embodies man the aspiring seed and God the all-nourishing Fruit.

EA 25. *11 July 1977, 10:00 p.m. — St Paul's Chapel, Columbia University, New York.*

26. ILLUMINATION

The animal world, the human world and the divine world: the world of destruction, the world of possession and the world of illumination.

Destruction is a very complicated term. In the animal world, destruction is at times necessary for survival. But otherwise, destruction is a negative force, a force of night, which is not at all encouraging, helpful or fruitful. Even the thought-world, which is so helpful in the human life, can be totally destructive. We do not need others to destroy us. One unhealthy, uncomely thought is enough to destroy our mental poise, and when we lose our mental poise, we lose everything.

When we breathe in, we breathe in many tiny creations of God. In order to live we have to breathe in, and they have to be our victims. When they are killed, the kind heart in us, on the strength of its oneness, should feel miserable. But when we enter into the deeper realm we see that this so-called destruction is not destruction at all. In God's Cosmic Plan this is the only way we can continue our present-day life. At the same time, this so-called destruction is a step ahead for those little creatures of God, for the soul evolves through the process of death and rebirth.

In the world of possession, we possess in order to enjoy. But while possessing we make discriminations. We want this; we do not want that. Because of our sense of separativity, we prefer this thing to that, but we prefer it in our human way. We prefer the things that stimulate us or the things that give us immediate joy and satisfaction. But in the case of God, there is no discrimination. He sees everything as His own, and inside everything He feels tremendous utility and necessity.

We want to possess the world, but our capacity of receptivity is so limited that we have to make a choice between this and that. In God's case, He does not make a choice, He does not have a preference; He possesses everything. He wants to bring to the fore His own Divinity which He has implanted in each creation of His. Even the destructive forces of ignorance have some light in them. So God wants to bring to the fore the infinitesimal light that even the ignorance-forces have. Like God, we also have to see the divinity in the ignorance-forces. Let us not see the outer world as such; let us not pay all attention to the outer body, which may not be divine. We will not deal with the outer body of the creation; we will deal only with the divinity, the inner reality of the creation, and then transform the body-reality so that it becomes as perfect as the soul-reality.

In the divine world, illumination is perfection. This illumination will never reject the possession-world or the destruction-world. It can easily house the possession-world and the destruction-world inside itself. When it enters into the destruction-world, it brings to the fore energy, for destruction has tremendous energy. It brings to the fore the energy-aspect of God's creation, and then utilises it for a divine purpose. When it enters into the possession-world, it possesses everything; it does not exclude anything. It brings to the fore the essence of divinity which is in everything. When the Divine comes forward, even the outer body can easily be transformed. The illumination-world does not exclude either the possession-world or the destruction-world. Illumination is the world of acceptance.

God has accepted the whole world for His own Satisfaction. But His Satisfaction is unlike our satisfaction. Our satisfaction is to claim and possess, to say, "This is mine; this is what I have." In God's case, He always sees His creation and His own Existence as one. In our case, possession always involves somebody else or something else. We say, "I am the possessor, and you are the possession." Then we feel that we are superior to our possession, for we can do anything we want with it. But God feels that He and His possessions are one and the same; they are equal.

Sometimes the possession will stand against the possessor or the creator. The parents are the creators of their children. When the children grow older and enter into adolescence, often they rebel. The possession, the creation, can become strong and go beyond the vision of the creator. In God's case, with His Vision He creates something, and if that creation goes beyond His Vision-Reality, He does not feel sad or miserable. On the contrary, this is what He actually wants. In His Vision-world He sees one Reality, but within this Reality there are many realities fully blossomed. In our case, if we get what we want, we are satisfied for a while. But if we get one cent more than we wanted, we are not satisfied, because that very thing we did not want. We want to possess, but if one thing more or one thing less than what we wanted comes, we are not satisfied, because our desire is such that we want the thing exactly the way our mind has conceived it. In God's case, even if it is not the same amount, He gets tremendous joy, because as soon as He projects His Vision, He is satisfied. In our case, after we have projected our will, we expect a certain kind of result, and if the result does not come up to our expectation, we feel miserable. In God's case, His projection itself is more than enough for His Satisfaction.

Destruction is at times necessary not only for survival, but to bring to the fore dynamic energy which is now being utilised in a destructive way. Otherwise, the world of lethargy and somnolence will cover the soul's indomitable energy. Possession itself is not bad, but we have to know what to possess. We have to know that the things that we really need are duty, beauty, light and delight. These things we have to bring to the fore. We will possess not the things that will possess us even while we are possessing them, but the things that will sing the song of oneness. Illumination is the acceptance of everything — destruction, possession, everything — but only for the sake of transformation. We have to accept, bring to the fore and transform.

The mind is now in the human world, the temptation-world. The eyes see something beautiful and immediately tempt the mind to go and grasp it. The ears hear something beautiful and immediately tempt the mind to go and grasp it. Each part of the body is subject to temptation and is assailed by temptation. Then it requires other parts of the being to come to its rescue and grab what is tempting it.

The illumination-world immediately will come in and grasp everything. Inside the temptation-world there will be a constant battle, a tug-of-war between the temptation itself and the illumination. The temptation wants to expand its own boundary, but even when it expands it is still not satisfied, because temptation is followed by frustration. So it looks around to seek abiding satisfaction here, there, everywhere. Then, when it sees illumination, finally it surrenders, for it sees that illumination is the answer.

Illumination encompasses the destruction-world, the possession-world and the temptation-world. We should always try to aim at illumination to save our earth-bound life from the destruction-world, and to transform our earth-bound life into the Heaven-free world.

EA 26. *12 July 1977, 8:15 a.m. — Jamaica High School Track, Jamaica, New York.*

27. EXPECTATION

Expectation is frustration, especially when I want to possess the world. Expectation is frustration, especially when I want to lord it over the world. Expectation is frustration, especially when I want the world to surrender to my will.

Expectation has its justification when I love the world and want the world to offer me a gratitude-heart. Expectation has its justification when I pray to God for the betterment, for the transformation, for the illumination of the world and want the world to offer me a gratitude-heart. Expectation has its justification when I sincerely, devotedly and unreservedly try to elevate the earth-consciousness according to my capacity and want the world to offer me a gratitude-heart.

Expectation is nothing short of satisfaction when I wait devotedly, soulfully and unconditionally for God's choice Hour to arrive to liberate, illumine, transform, perfect and fulfil me. Expectation is satisfaction when I feel in the inmost recesses of my heart that God is not only my sovereign Lord, the Absolute Supreme, but also my Friend, my eternal Friend and only Friend. Expectation is satisfaction, especially when I know that God has done everything for me in the inner world. This discovery of mine is founded on my faith, my inner faith in Him, not because He is all Love for me, but because I have realised something that is infinitely more significant. My realisation is this: my God, my Lord Supreme, my eternal Friend, does everything in and through me. He is expanding and enlarging His own cosmic Vision in and through me. When I realise my expectation of what He has done for me and what He is to me, my life has its soulful purpose and fruitful delight.

When I use the human in me to serve any purpose, my expectation becomes frustration. When I use the divine in me to serve any purpose, my expectation has its justification. At that time expectation itself is justification. But when I use my Lord Supreme, my eternal Friend, to fulfil something, my expectation is satisfaction, for the expectation is the Vision-Light, the satisfaction is the Reality-Delight. They are one and inseparable.

EA 27. *12 July 1977, 1:50 p.m. — Dag Hammarskjold Auditorium, United Nations, New York.*

28. OBEDIENCE WAS MY WAY OF LIFE

Obedience was my way of life. Many, many, many years ago my Beloved Supreme once came to me and said, "My son, pray. You must pray. From now on you must pray to Me regularly." I obeyed my Beloved Supreme and I started praying.

A few years later my Beloved Supreme came to me and said, "My son, meditate. I want you to meditate. From now on you must meditate regularly every day." I obeyed my Beloved Supreme.

Then one day He came to me and said, "My son, do you see any change, any improvement, anything new in your life?"

I said, "I do see."

Then He said, "What is it?"

I told Him, "I will be very glad if You tell me the changes and improvements that I have made, for I may make a mistake. Whatever You say I will gladly accept as absolutely true."

My Beloved Supreme was very pleased with me. He said, "Since you have started praying, you have been feeling your closeness to Me. Since you have started meditating, you have been feeling My closeness to you. When you pray you feel your closeness to Me, and when you meditate you feel My closeness to you.

"Something more: when you pray you see My Kindness-aspect and My Compassion-aspect, and when you meditate you see My Beauty-aspect and My Fruitfulness-aspect. When you pray I am kind and compassionate to you, and when you meditate I am beautiful and fruitful to you. These four qualities or attributes of Mine are of tremendous importance. Unless I am kind and compassionate to you, why would I show you My Beauty and My Fruitfulness? Why should I show the things that I have, the things that I embody? Because you pray, you see My Kindness-aspect and My Compassion-aspect, and because you meditate you see My Beauty-aspect and My Fruitfulness-aspect.

"Something more you will feel. When you pray, from now on you will feel that you need Me only, and when you meditate you will feel that I need you only. Right now it is impossible for you to believe that I need you only, because in every way I am superior to you. You think that you know who you are and who I am. But a day will come when you will realise that we are one and inseparable. Until then it will be difficult for you to feel that I embody the finite aspect of life and still hold the Infinite aspect. I know that inside the finite aspect is the Infinite, and inside the Infinite aspect is the finite, but still you have not realised that.

"When I say that I need you only, you have to know what I mean. You may say, 'There are millions and billions and trillions of people on earth, so how is it that He cares only for me and not for others?' But you have to feel that 'you' means your extended, expanded part. Your eyes have become larger than the largest, your arms have become longer than the longest. Your whole existence has expanded and enlarged, and all other human beings are only your extended, expanded reality — part of your own existence. Therefore, when you meditate and feel that I need you only, it means that I need you as a universal Reality.

"If you keep on praying and meditating, then you are obeying Me. And if you obey Me, there is nothing that I shall not do for you. I shall always do everything for you if you pray and meditate. When you pray you will feel that My Life-breath is embodying you, and when you meditate you will feel that your life-breath is embodying Me. Prayer and meditation are of tremendous importance. But there will come a time when you will become inseparably one with My Consciousness, finite and Infinite, universal and transcendental. At that time you may give up the prayer-aspect, for the meditation-aspect will embody everything. In the prayer-aspect there is some feeling of superiority and inferiority. If you regard Me as the Lord Supreme, then it will be difficult for you to accept Me as your only Friend, your Eternity's Friend. At that time I embody My Absolute aspect, My aspect of sovereignty and lordship. But there may come a time when you will feel that I am your only Friend. At that time you need not approach Me as the Lord Supreme and pray to Me. Your prayer-life may come to an end.

"It is difficult or impossible for the prayer-life to embody the meditation-life, but the meditation-life can easily embody the prayer-life. Right now you should both pray and meditate. But eventually, when you become highly advanced, on the verge of realisation or realised, then you can give up praying, for in meditation you can easily get the fruits of prayer along with the meditation-fruits, which are all-important."

EA 28. *13 July 1977, 7:30 a.m. — Jamaica High School Track, Jamaica, New York.*

29. YOU AND YOUR PERFECTION

You are telling me that you are perfect. Then show me the vitality-flood of your vital. I see you have it. Thank you.

You are telling me that you are perfect. Then show me the serenity-river of your mind. I see you have it. Thank you.

You are telling me that you are perfect. Then show me the divinity-sea of your heart. I see you have it. Thank you.

You are telling me that you are perfect. Then show me a purity-drop of your body. I see you have it. Thank you.

Indeed, you are right. Indeed, you are perfect.

EA 29. *13 July 1977, 9:35 p.m. — Yoga-Life Perfection, New York.*

30. YOGA AND ONENESS

Yoga is conscious oneness.

Yoga is my conscious oneness with what I have and what I am. What I have is God-realisation. What I am is God-Delight.

Yoga is conscious oneness with God's eternal Duty. Yoga is conscious oneness with God's infinite Beauty.

Yoga is conscious oneness with earth's insufficiency-cry. Yoga is conscious oneness with Heaven's sufficiency-smile.

Yoga is conscious oneness with man's surrender-perfection. Yoga is conscious oneness with God's Acceptance-Satisfaction.

Yoga is conscious oneness with God's Vision-Boat. Yoga is conscious oneness with God's Reality-Shore.

EA 30. *13 July 1977, 9:37 p.m. — Yoga-Life Perfection, New York.*

31. HATHA YOGA

O Yoga of the sun and the moon, I sincerely appreciate you, I unmistakably admire you.

O *Ha,* O sun, O sun-world, O sun-power, O sun-god, I adore you.

O *Tha,* O moon, O moon-world, O moon-shower, O moon-goddess, I adore you.

O *Hatha Yoga,* you are preparing for me a strong body, a sound vital, an illumining mind and a pure heart. From your valuable gifts I shall receive inspiration to take three long strides towards my life's integral perfection and my Lord's complete satisfaction: concentration, meditation and contemplation.

Concentration will penetrate the ignorance-world. Meditation will sit on the snow-capped mountain peak. Contemplation will join the divine lover and the Supreme Beloved in their oneness-dance.

EA 31. *13 July 1977, 9:39 p.m. — Yoga-Life Perfection, New York.*

32. INTUITION

Intuition, you are great. You run faster than the fastest. You have the lightning speed. You have free access to the past realities and to the present realities. You are great because you have lightning speed. Your lightning speed frightens the weak, encourages the strong, confuses the foolish and pleases the wise.

O intuition, you are really great. You have the capacity to know the world, inner and outer. But alas, you do not have the capacity to change the world. If you want to change the world, then you will have to go to realisation. It will not only fulfil your desire, but will also grant you another boon: satisfaction in God-realisation, satisfaction in God-revelation, satisfaction in God-manifestation.

EA 32. *13 July 1977, 9:41 p.m. — Yoga-Life Perfection, New York.*

33. PERFECTION

Perfection: what is it? It is an ever-transcending reality. Perfection is to reach Divinity's feet with humanity's heart. Perfection is to change the life-style of the finite world and to manifest the life-style of the Infinite.

Perfection is not self-justification. Perfection is not self-proclamation. Perfection is not self-annihilation. Perfection is God-invitation, God-adoration and God-satisfaction.

Perfection is to have sterling faith in God's constant Compassion. Perfection is to have staunch faith in man's crying aspiration.

Who says that perfection on earth is self-delusion? Perfection is God-glorification in man.

Who says that perfection is a far cry? No, it is nearer than the heart-beat, nearer than the life-breath.

Something more: perfection embodies God the aspiring, evolving, transcending, illumining and fulfilling man.

EA 33. *13 July 1977, 9:43 p.m. — Yoga-Life Perfection, New York.*

34. IF YOU HAVE, THEN COME TO ME

If you have a disturbing thought, then come to me. I shall give you my challenging will.

If you have an impure mind, then come to me. I shall give you my pure heart.

If you have an uncomely body, then come to me. I shall give you my beautiful soul.

If you have an unsatisfied life, then come to me. I shall give you my satisfied God.

EA 34. *13 July 1977, 9:45 p.m. — Yoga-Life Perfection, New York.*

35. I AM PRIVILEGED

I am privileged that God has granted me a human incarnation. It is only in the human life that I can realise Him, reveal Him and manifest Him unreservedly and unconditionally.

I am privileged that ignorance-dream does not dare to intimidate me, because it sees God and God's constant Protection around me.

I am privileged that my heart loves my Lord Supreme infinitely more than my mind can ever imagine.

I am privileged that my Lord Supreme Himself has asked me to offer Him a silent prayer and a soulful meditation early in the morning before I enter into the hustle and bustle of life. My silent prayer is this: "O Lord Supreme, do accept my surrender-life." My soulful meditation is this: "O Lord Supreme, do enter into my gratitude-heart and remain seated there."

I am privileged that my Lord Supreme discusses His Cosmic Plans with me in Heaven, and I am privileged that He has made me a faithful representative of His to execute His Will here on earth.

I am privileged that at every moment God loves me more than I deserve, He speaks to me more than I deserve, He gives me more than I deserve. In every way He does things for me, says things to me and dreams in and through me infinitely more than I shall ever deserve.

I am privileged that I fully and soulfully claim Him as my own, very own, my own Eternity's own.

EA 35. *14 July 1977, 12:40 p.m. — Sri Chinmoy Centre, Jamaica, New York.*

36. I AM HELPLESS

O Lord Supreme, I am helpless. You have given me the eyes to see and the heart to feel, but You have not given me the arms to do the needful, to change what I see and feel has to be changed.

You have Your sons and daughters. Your sons have made such friendship with impurity that I find it impossible to put an end to their friendship. Your daughters have made such friendship with insecurity that I find it impossible to put an end to their friendship. What is worse, Your sons not only unconsciously, but also consciously, even deliberately, throw their poison, their impurity, into the aspiring hearts and lives of Your daughters. Your daughters consciously and deliberately throw their insecurity-ant into Your sons' lives. When impurity enters into Your daughters from Your sons, the limited purity of Your daughters disappears. When the insecurity of Your daughters enters into Your sons, Your sons' limited courage disappears. This does not mean that women have no impurity; they do have impurity, but in comparison to men they have less. And men do have insecurity, but in comparison to women, they have less.

Your sons feel that aggression — physical, vital and mental — is man's proper role. Your daughters feel that frustration — physical, vital and mental — is woman's proper role. Man's aggression destroys the mind before the mind is aware of aggression's attack. Man's aggression destroys man's vital the moment it enters into the vital. Man's body is destroyed the moment it hears the very name of aggression. Man's heart is destroyed at the very sight of aggression. Yet Your sons like aggression, love aggression and have become inseparable friends with aggression.

Your daughters enjoy frustration more than anything else in their life. They are frustrated because their teeming desires are not fulfilled; they are frustrated because their desires are fulfilled. When their desires are not fulfilled, they feel that they are beggar-women. When their desires are fulfilled, they feel that God is giving something more important to other human beings, but because they have desired and asked for the wrong things, they are now in the frustration-world. They feel that they should have asked for something else; they should have made a correct choice. Or they should not have had any desire; then there would have been no frustration. Because they asked for the wrong thing, they feel miserable. Because they asked for anything at all, they feel equally miserable. Again, if they had not asked to have their desires fulfilled, they would have felt miserable. So frustration is their lot. When they have their desires fulfilled, they are frustrated. When they do not ask You to fulfil their desires, they are also frustrated.

Everything needs a place, either for its safety or just because everything has a supreme need for a place to rest, to have perfect shelter. Men find a safe place for their aggression inside women; women find a safe place, a resting place, for their frustration inside men. Man offers his aggression-injection to woman's heart and woman offers her frustration-injection to man's life.

My Lord Supreme, I am helpless because I see the impurity-flood and the cannon-shot of aggression of Your sons; and I am helpless because I see the insecurity-river and the frustration-panther of Your daughters. These discouraging, destructive and deplorable qualities, nay, capacities, of men and women are destroying Your sons and daughters right in front of my compassion-vision and my realisation-reality.

O Lord Supreme, if I ask You, request You, to give more capacity to the men and women so that they can overcome their shortcomings, You just tell me that You have already given them the necessary capacity to conquer these unaspiring, discouraging, destructive forces. You have already given them the capacity, O Lord Supreme, but do me a favour: give them more capacity, not because they deserve it, not because they themselves feel the need of it, but because I feel that I am unable to help them. I tried with them, I prayed for them, but I could not help them. At that time weakness was their conscious and unconscious strength. But there shall come a time when they will have no weakness whatsoever.

I was the inspirer, I was the server, I was the lover of this new vision that has the power in it to change the face of the world. Vision without power is no vision. What good is it to see when you cannot change? Again, if you don't see what you have to change, what are you going to change? It is good to see, it is better to change, and it is best, after you have made the change, to prolong this change, this perfection, indefinitely and eternally.

My Lord Supreme, You have given me the vision to see Your creation as it is. But do go one step ahead and give me the capacity and power to change the face of the world and fulfil You in Your own Way.

My Lord Supreme, this is the way one aspect of me has observed Your creation. But the lover in me observes Your creation in a different way. Since You have created the world, since it is Your creation, I am a hundred per cent one with the weaknesses of Your sons and daughters, with my loving concern-heart, serving life-breath and illumining soul-beauty.

EA 36. *14 July 1977, 12:45 p.m. — Sri Chinmoy Centre, Jamaica, New York.*

37. GET UP!

Get Up, O my body, get up! Don't sleep. You have slept for a long time. Don't sleep any more. Are you not ashamed of your life? Don't sleep. The goal is far, very far.

O my vital, stand up, stand up! You have been sitting for a long time. It is high time for you to stand up. Stand up! Are you not ashamed of your life? The goal is far, very far. Don't sit any more. Stand up.

O my mind, run, run! You have been standing in one place for a long time. The goal is far, very far. You have to run towards the destination. Are you not ashamed of your life, standing in one place when you know perfectly well that the goal is a far cry? Run, run towards the destination! Don't stand in one place. Run towards the destined goal.

O my heart, run the fastest! Are you not ashamed of your life? You are supposed to run the fastest, but you are running slowly, very slowly. The goal is still a far cry. Are you not ashamed of your life? Slowly you are running. Are you not ashamed of your speed? From now on, you have to run the fastest, O my heart. Then only will you be satisfied when you reach your goal. If you run slowly, it will take you millions of years. Also, while running slowly you may lose your enthusiasm one day and give up on your way to your destination. Therefore, run the fastest, O my heart, and reach the destination. See the face of your goal. Become one, inseparably one, with your goal.

O body of mine, O vital of mine, O mind of mine, O heart of mine, from now on feel that each moment you lose here on earth, each moment you neglect, means a year of delay, a year of frustration, a year of failure, has been added to your life. Therefore, get up, O my body; stand up, O my vital; run, O my mind; run the fastest, O my heart! Each second you can either build a new life of hope, promise, realisation and perfection or you can destroy what you have right now in a very small measure: aspiration. Do not destroy your aspiration; only build the edifice of your hope-light, promise-height, realisation-oneness and perfection-delight.

EA 37. *14 July 1977, 5:35 p.m. — Sri Chinmoy Centre, Jamaica, New York.*

38. DON'T SUFFER!

Don't suffer! O my body, O my vital, O my mind, O my heart, do not suffer. Do not cherish suffering. Don't act like a fool. Don't think that your suffering is going to accelerate your spiritual progress. Don't think that your suffering will bring God closer to you sooner than at once. Don't think that your suffering is the only way, the sure way, for you to make progress. Never!

Look at the plus and minus factors of your suffering. The plus factors: Your suffering adds to your fear, your uncontrollable fear. Your suffering adds to your disproportionate rebellious attitude in the long run. Your suffering adds to your poisonous frustration. Your suffering adds to your slow and steady destruction. The minus factors: O body, vital, mind and heart of mine, your suffering takes away all that your Beloved Lord Supreme has granted you. Out of His infinite Bounty He has given you joy, He has given you His Concern, He has given you His Compassion, He has given you His Oneness. But you cherished and treasured suffering; therefore, all His gifts have been stolen. By whom? By your own suffering. So suffering is not the way. It takes away from you all the precious gifts that God has given you. One by one the suffering-thief robs you of the most precious, most coveted gifts that God has given you: His own Peace, His own Love, His own Bliss, His own Concern, His own Oneness.

From now on, try to catch the suffering-thief red-handed and bring the thief to your Beloved Supreme. Once the thief is caught, once you have offered the thief to the right person, once the right person, the Beloved Supreme, knows that you do not want to be robbed by anyone either in your inner family or in your outer family, once He knows that you do not want to be robbed either by the members of your own inner existence or by the members of the outer world, at that time your Beloved Supreme grants you once again, out of His infinite Bounty, His Concern, His Love, His Joy, His Oneness, His Compassion and His Pride in boundless measure.

So, O seeker, in body, vital, mind and heart, do not cherish suffering even for a fleeting second. Suffering is not the answer; suffering is only a question mark which will never be satisfied with any answer we give. Suffering is the question mark that defies all answers. Even if God answers the question, even then the mind will not accept the answer as the correct one.

Suffering is not the right way. From now on, only grow in joy and self-confidence. This self-confidence comes from your surrendered oneness-will with your Beloved Supreme. You want confidence and you will get confidence the moment your surrendered oneness with the Will of the Supreme is perfect. Before that, there is no confidence; there can be no confidence in you or in anything else.

So, O seeker, with your body, vital, mind and heart, accept the divine gifts; cherish them, treasure them, increase them. How will you increase them? Through conscious self-giving with utmost gratitude to your Beloved Supreme. If you can smile soulfully, all the divine gifts that you have got from the Supreme are bound to increase. If you can sing in silence soulfully, all the divine gifts that you have already received from the Supreme are bound to increase. If you can dance devotedly and soulfully inside your gratitude-heart, then all the divine gifts that you have received so far are bound to increase. Something more: you will not only get blessingful gifts, fruitful gifts from Him, but you will also get the Creator and the Possessor of the gifts, the Supreme Himself. He who created the gifts for you, He who possessed the gifts for you, will be more than ready and eager to be possessed by you. He wants you to claim His possessions as your own, very own. Then, once you have claimed His possessions as your own, He will come and stand in front of you and say, "My child, you have accepted My gifts, which are My creations. I am so pleased with you. Now accept Me. I am all yours." So claim all the divine gifts that you have been offered by the Supreme. Claim them individually and collectively as your own, very own. Then the real owner of the gifts will come to you and offer Himself to you to be claimed by you constantly and eternally.

EA 38. *14 July 1977, 5:45 p.m — Sri Chinmoy Centre, Jamaica, New York.*

39. DISCIPLES, FOLLOWERS, ADMIRERS AND WELL-WISHERS

"My Lord Supreme, do tell me the difference between a disciple and a follower."

"My son, the difference is this: a disciple is he who constantly thinks only of his Master's need. He feels that his very existence on earth is for his Master alone, only for his Master. When the Master asks him to do something for him, he says, 'Master, I have already done it.' As a matter of fact, he *has* done it, for intuitively he has felt the Master's need long before the Master has asked him on the outer plane to do something for him.

"A follower is he who wants to do what the Master asks him to do, but he will tell his Master, 'O Master, I will do it, but please give me some time. You have asked me to do something, so definitely I will do it, but what you have asked is not an easy task; therefore, I may take some time. But I assure you, I shall do it. Have faith in me. I shall not disappoint you, not to speak of deserting you. If I do it immediately, I may not succeed, so give me some time. I shall do it without fail.'"

"My Lord Supreme, please tell me the difference between an admirer and a well-wisher."

"My son, here is the difference: an admirer is he who admires the Master at a distance. He does not want to be involved with the Master's practical needs. He does not want to be close to the Master or near the Master, for he thinks that his nearness will be exploited by the Master, or he thinks that if he remains near the Master he will see the Master's shortcomings and lessen his admiration for his Master. He will admire from a distance, but he will not approach the Master, for the Master may ask him for a favour which he may not be in a position or have the willingness to fulfil. Again, he is afraid that if the Master behaves in a human way, then the little admiration for the Master that he does have may not last. So he is afraid of his own life, of his own security, of his own standard, of his own realisation. He does not want to associate with the Master closely, for he feels that the Master in his dream-world is one thing, whereas the Master in the reality-world will be a different thing.

"A well-wisher is he who knows about a spiritual figure and entertains a good opinion of him. He reads about the Master in the newspaper, or sees him on television or hears about him on the radio, and he thinks that the Master is a good person. But the Master, the spiritual figure, never expects anything from a well-wisher; therefore, he and the well-wisher remain at a distance."

"My Lord Supreme, do tell me something more about them."

"My son, when the Master sails his boat towards the Golden Shore, the disciple remains in the boat, fully one with the Master's will. He looks at the Master's movements and observes how he is piloting the boat, and all the time he is praying for the Master's inner and outer success and victory. He is all eagerness to see the Master's victory. He sleeplessly observes the Master's way of piloting the boat, and is all the time learning from the Master how the Master pilots the boat.

"The follower sits in the boat. He feels that just because he has told the Master that he is following his path, he has given his fee, so he can remain safe. His promise itself is the fee; therefore, it is the Master's bounden duty to take him to the Golden Shore. Since he has bought the ticket, since he has got a seat inside the boat, he feels that he does not have to watch; the boat will bring him to his destination. On his own he does not have to remain awake; he does not have to be of any help or service — inner or outer. He can remain asleep, he can enjoy himself, but it is the Master's bounden duty to do the needful, because he has accepted the disciple.

"An admirer is he who comes right up to the boat but is afraid to enter. He is afraid that if he takes the journey, some water animals may capsize the boat or some doubt-hurricane may blow him out of the boat or destroy the boat. He is afraid that he will not be able to survive the journey.

"The admirer watches the journey from the shore. He watches the Master and the disciples and followers in the boat. The Master is navigating from this shore to another shore. The admirer sees and admires, but he is afraid. He thinks that the boat will capsize, so he does not enter into the boat.

"A well-wisher does not even come to see the boat take off on its journey. He hears from others, or reads in the newspaper, or hears on the radio or television that the Master has embarked on a journey to an unhorizoned land. If the Master succeeds, well and good. If he fails, who cares? A well-wisher is nothing in the outer world but a fair-weather friend. If the Master succeeds, he will say, 'Oh, I know him. He is so great, so good, so kind.' If he fails, he will say, 'Oh, I know him. He is useless; therefore, I did not want to follow his path.' So this is the difference between a disciple, a follower, an admirer and a well-wisher."

EA 39. *14 July 1977, 8:40 p.m. — Martin Van Buren High School, Hollis, New York.*

40. RELIANCE

I rely on God's Promise; I do not rely on my own feelings. I rely only on God's Promise; I do not rely on my own assessment of myself. Quite often I feel an emptiness inside me. When I feel that I am empty, at that time I feel lonely, I feel miserable, I feel not only helpless and hopeless but also sure that I am going to destruction itself. When I think of myself, I see frustration within and without. Fear and jealousy, insecurity and doubt, disobedience and arrogance play in front of me an undivine game. The name of that game is ingratitude.

If I rely on their assessment of my life, if I rely on them, if I take them as my confidants, if I take them as true members of my family, then I am totally ruined. So I rely only on my God's Promise that He will teach me how to swim across the ignorance-sea. My Lord's Promise to me is so clear, vivid, illumining and fulfilling. He told me that I am destined to become a perfect instrument of His. He told me that I am destined to swim in the sea of Light and Delight and eventually teach others — my little brothers and sisters — how to swim in the sea of Light and Delight.

I do not rely on my physical height, on my material or earthly achievement-heights; they are misleading. I see that I am tall, but in comparison to whom? To children. I see clearly that I am so tall, but only when I stand in front of children. When a giant stands in front of me, I become a tiny little ant, a pigmy, in comparison to the giant's height. So my earthly height is such that it does not give me abiding satisfaction. When I am with children, my height satisfies me because I am much taller than they are. But when I am with grown-ups, giants, I am not aware of my achievements. I can extol myself to the skies for my achievements and feel that I have achieved something great and sublime; but when I look around, I see right in front of my nose that there is someone who has far surpassed me in that very field. So if I rely on my achievements to give me strength, security, confidence and assurance, I am misled and misguided. But when I think of my Lord's Height in me, when I try to see and feel it, I see that He has not only the tallest Height but also the ever-transcending Height. Here on the physical plane I can reach a certain height and then it is over. On the physical plane, material plane, I attain something; then it comes to an end. But on the inner plane, when I think of my Lord Supreme, everything that He has and everything that He is, is not only measureless, but also ever-transcending. Here in the outer world my height always has a limit, but there in the inner world my Lord's Height, my Lord's Achievements, are all unlimited.

What is my Lord's Promise to me? His Promise to me is that what He has and what He is, is all for me: His Height, His inner Height, His real Height, His real Achievements, are all for me. This is His Promise. So I rely on His Promise and do not rely on my own little capacities and achievements. My own little capacities do not satisfy me. Even if one satisfies me for a second, I see tremendous weakness in that capacity, for there is always somebody else who is endowed with infinitely more of that capacity than I have.

Reliance means satisfaction. When I rely on myself I cannot have total satisfaction. But when I rely on my Lord Supreme, when I rely on His Promise, it is simple. He will make me, like Himself, another God, with Infinity, Eternity and Immortality at my constant disposal. In me He sees the perfect prototype of His own Reality. His Promise is to make of me another Reality exactly like His own, so that He can play with me, sing with me and dance with me throughout Eternity.

When He promises to make me into an exact image of His own Reality, this does not mean that inseparable oneness is lacking. No, inseparable oneness is there, but the One projects Himself into two so that He can enjoy the Cosmic Game. In the outer plane, the human mind will see separativity in spite of inseparable oneness in the inner world. But the heart will feel that the One has divided Himself into two to taste the cosmic Delight. When oneness is divided into two halves, each half brings in newness; each half offers constant newness, ever-illumining, ever-fulfilling newness to the other.

So I shall rely only on my Lord's Promise, and not on what I have and what I am. I do not trust, I cannot trust myself for I do not trust the members of my inner family: the body, vital, mind and heart. They have deceived me and I have deceived them. But my Lord Supreme has never deceived me and I have never deceived Him. Therefore, I rely on Him only, and He relies on me. I do not rely on the members of my earthly-existence-family; neither will I allow them to rely on me. My reality, my confidence, my assurance, my very existence is founded upon my reliance on my Beloved Supreme alone.

EA 40. *14 July 1977, 8:53 p.m. — Martin Van Buren High School, Hollis, New York.*

41. IT IS NOT ENOUGH

Body, what are you looking for? You are looking for comfort. Don't you know that comfort is nothing but darkness and blindness in disguise? Vital, what are you looking for? You are looking for pleasure. Don't you know that pleasure is ignorance-sea in disguise? Mind, what are you looking for? You are looking for a complacent life. Don't you know that complacency is nothing short of the beginning of self-destruction? O heart, what are you looking for? You are looking for security. But you cherish your feebleness; you cherish your attachment-life. You look here, there and everywhere only to lead a life of attachment. Don't you know that the life of attachment is nothing short of immediate frustration? Frustration is bound to be followed by destruction, and destruction is death in disguise.

O body, in order to develop more of a sense of responsibility day in and day out, you have to pray for God to shower His choice Compassion on you. O vital, in order to develop more simplicity, you have to pray for God to grant you His constant blessingful Concern. O mind, in order to develop more sincerity, you have to pray for God to grant you His immediate Peace. In peace you will develop and increase your sincerity. O heart, in order to free yourself from attachment, in order to enlarge your vision, in order to have a palace of wideness, a spacious building with a spacious room inside for you to converse with the Lord Supreme, you have to pray to Him.

O my body, your sense of responsibility is not enough. You need more responsibility. O my vital, your sense of simplicity is not enough. You definitely need more simplicity. O my mind, your sense of sincerity is not enough. You need, without fail, more sincerity. O my heart, your sense of purity is not enough. You unmistakably need more purity. O members of my inner family, if you do not have responsibility, simplicity, sincerity and purity in abundant measure, then my life's journey will end in utter failure. Therefore, I beg of you to have a greater sense of responsibility, simplicity, sincerity and purity.

Unless all of you develop more of a sense of responsibility, simplicity, sincerity and purity, the Supreme in me will remain unfulfilled. And each day that my God remains unfulfilled, I see and feel that my promise to God, my beloved God, is dining with frustration, destruction and death. Each day I feel that I am disappointing my Beloved Supreme; I am even deserting Him. Because of you, O body, vital, mind and heart, I am unable to please the Supreme, my Beloved Supreme.

O body, if you do not abide by my request; O vital, if you do not see eye to eye with me; O mind, if you fail to please me; O heart, if you do not please the Supreme the way I want you to please Him, then there will be no option, no choice. God will, out of His infinite Bounty, give me new instruments, instruments that are more willing, more eager, more obedient to His Will. And if you fail the Supreme in me in this incarnation, then rest assured that you will have to wait for countless years, if not indefinitely, before you will be granted another opportunity. Therefore, O body, vital, mind and heart, do not miss this golden opportunity. The golden day awaits your life, my life and God's Life every day. You fulfil the Supreme in me and I shall fulfil the Supreme in you. You give me what I need and I shall give you what you need. What you desperately need is satisfaction. You give me obedience-oneness and I shall give you satisfaction-perfection.

EA 41. *15 July 1977, 7:40 a.m. — Jamaica High School Track, Jamaica, New York.*

42. AWARENESS, DEVOTEDNESS, SOULFULNESS AND SELFLESSNESS

Awareness, devotedness, soulfulness and selflessness: these are my lifelong friends. Awareness has transformed my animal life into human life. Devotedness has transformed my human life into divine life. Soulfulness has lengthened my divine life, and selflessness has immortalised my divine life.

Awareness has discovered all the higher worlds. Devotedness has discovered all the inner worlds. Soulfulness has discovered God's universal Life. Selflessness has discovered God's transcendental Life.

Awareness has a special connection with God the Creator. Awareness has pleased God the Creator in a special way. Devotedness has a special connection with God the Saviour. Devotedness has pleased God the Saviour in a special way. Soulfulness has a special connection with God the Liberator. Soulfulness has pleased God the Liberator in a special way. Selflessness has a special connection with God the Supreme Singer, God the Supreme Dancer and God the Supreme Lover. Selflessness has pleased God the Supreme Singer, God the Supreme Dancer and God the Supreme Lover in a special way.

On the physical plane my awareness-friend has made me smart, my devotedness-friend has made me bright, my soulfulness-friend has made me pure, my selflessness-friend has made me sure. My awareness-friend stands at my heart's door and prevents ignorance from entering into my heart-room. My devotedness-friend tells me always to be thankful and grateful to the Supreme Pilot within me for what He has unconditionally done for me. My soulfulness-friend helps me identify myself with God the Creator, God the creation, God the One and God the many, to enjoy supreme oneness with the Beloved Supreme. My selflessness-friend helps me always to become consciously part and parcel of God the creation, and a surrendered instrument of God the Creator. My selflessness-friend tells me that today's unrealised and unfulfilled man is definitely going to be tomorrow's realised and fulfilled man.

The consciousness-ladder has four unique rungs: awareness, devotedness, soulfulness and selflessness. The consciousness-ladder that unites earth's cry and Heaven's Smile is for the seeker in me. When I step on the first rung, awareness, my ignorance-friend of the hoary past looks at me and is amazed, totally amazed, that I have stepped on the awareness-rung. Finally it disappears in utter frustration and failure. When I step on the second rung of the consciousness-ladder, devotedness, the ignorance-dream that once upon a time tortured my very being and existence is no more. The ignorance-dream cries for transformation. It cries to me to transform it into wisdom-reality. When I step on the soulfulness-rung, the world of frustration, worries, anxieties and utter failure stands before me for its improvement, progress and radical change. When I stand, finally, on the selflessness-rung, I become inseparably one with what the world has and with what the world does not have. What the world has is an inner cry; what the world does not have is a soulful smile from the ever-transcending Heights.

There is only one outer world, and this outer world is my preparation-world, which is founded upon my own awareness, devotedness, soulfulness and selflessness.

EA 42. *15 July 1977, 12:50 p.m. — Dag Hammarskjold Auditorium, United Nations, New York.*

43. I DO NOT IMITATE; I DO NOT INITIATE

I do not imitate; I do not initiate. I do not imitate anything, I do not imitate anybody; for if I imitate, then I prevent my Beloved Supreme from revealing His new creation. At every moment He wants to create something new, something meaningful and something fruitful in and through me. I do not initiate anything on any plane, for I may make mistakes; I may commit deplorable blunders. I may mislead others.

I do not imitate; I do not initiate. I just concentrate, meditate and contemplate. I concentrate in order to pierce the ignorance-veil which has enveloped me. I meditate in order to liberate myself from ignorance-dream. I contemplate in order to remember what I did with my Beloved Supreme inside Him, around Him, within Him and without Him, long, long, long ago.

I concentrate in order to run the fastest towards my destined Goal, towards my Beloved Supreme. I meditate so that my Goal, my Beloved Supreme, can come to me sooner than at once. I contemplate so that my Lord Supreme and I will run together to find a place where we can meet and again resume our age-old marathon conversation.

I do not imitate; I do not initiate. I concentrate, I meditate and I contemplate. My concentration gives me the strength to fight against teeming ignorance. My meditation gives me poise amidst the turbulent weather of human life. My contemplation lets me always feel that my Lord Supreme, my

Beloved Supreme, is hearing my aspiration-cry, my heart's inmost cry.

EA 43. *15 July 1977, 10:00 p.m. — North Shore Community Arts Center, Great Neck, New York.*

44. WHY DO I HIDE?

"My Lord Supreme, why is it that at times I want to hide from You? Why is it that at times I desperately try to hide my thoughts from You? Why? Why? Is it because I am afraid of You? Or is it because I love You and I feel that it will hurt You if You know my uncomely and impure thoughts on the physical plane? On the inner plane I know I will never be able to deceive You. On the outer plane, because of my clever mind, I feel that in a human way I shall be able to deceive You, because perhaps You are not aware of all the intricacies of human life. Anyway, do tell me why I want to hide myself from You and hide my thoughts from You."

"My child, to some extent it is true that you are afraid of Me. That is why you hide from Me. Again, to some extent it is true that you are afraid that it will hurt Me — that is to say, the human consciousness in Me — if I see that you are suffering from unhealthy thoughts. Being identified with you, I shall undoubtedly suffer. But the main reason is something else. You unconsciously, if not consciously, cherish the life of ignorance. You want to hide from Me because you know that although you are now consciously for the life of wisdom, still ignorance-life is dominating you and lording it over you. You cherish these thoughts because you feel that these are things that you can have, whereas divine thoughts, illumining thoughts, Heavenly thoughts, perhaps are all mental hallucinations. This is what you think: therefore, you unconsciously, if not consciously, cherish and treasure your undivine thoughts.

"But, My child, I wish to tell you that you must not be afraid of Me or feel that you will hurt Me. The divine in Me will never punish you. The divine in Me will never be hurt by your so-called shortcomings. You can get rid of these ignorant feelings, ideas and notions on the physical plane very easily. If you want to get rid of these forces, just think of Me as a wastepaper basket or a dustbin. On the physical plane, these are the two proper places for you to get rid of anything that is unwanted. If you want to get rid of these unhealthy thoughts on the spiritual plane, then soulfully and devotedly throw them into Me. Throw anything that you are suffering from into me. I am for your illumination, for your perfection, and I shall never remain satisfied unless I see your radical transformation.

"You have to feel that your shortcomings are My shortcomings. You are not afraid of yourself; you don't try to hide from yourself, because you know that it is you. Similarly, if you can think of Me as your enlarged, expanded reality, if you can feel that your arms are lengthened, that everything you have is expanded, and that in this expanded and enlarged consciousness you and I are one, then you will see that the things that have to be transformed in you are also shortcomings in Me.

"So do not be afraid of Me or fear that you will hurt Me in a human way. Think of Me as a wastepaper basket. Feel that I am that very thing: your universal Life, your transcendental Life. Why should you be afraid of Me? We are one, eternally one, inseparably one. The lesser in us is being illumined with the light of the greater, the more illumined, more fulfilling, more perfect and more divine."

EA 44. *16 July 1977, 8:30 a.m. — Jamaica High School Track, Jamaica, New York.*

45. I AM IN PREPARATION

I am in preparation. I am in preparation for a new dawn, a new morning and a new day. I shall consciously and forcefully bury my past experiences — experiences of failure, experiences of frustration, experiences of unworthiness. I shall bury them. I shall obliterate from my memory-tablet all the uncomely experiences, the unilluming experiences, that I have had so far in my life. I am in preparation for an ever-new life.

I know why I have failed, why I have disappointed my Beloved Supreme. I have failed because I have neglected my second-life, I have wasted my minute-life, I have ignored my hour-life. From now on, in each second-life of mine I shall see a reality-existence of ten years. In each minute-life of mine I shall see a reality-existence of forty years, and in each hour-life I shall see a reality-existence of a hundred years, countless years. Each time I do not properly use my second-life, minute-life and hour-life, I shall make myself feel that I am far, farther, farthest from my destined Goal. And each time I properly utilise my second-life, minute-life and hour-life, I shall undoubtedly make myself feel that my hour of God-realisation is fast approaching. I shall not have to force myself to feel this; it will be something spontaneous and automatic. I shall no longer ply my boat between hope-evening and frustration-night. I shall ply my boat only between promise-light and satisfaction-delight.

Because of my bondage-life, because of my desire-life, because of my finite life, I have failed my Beloved Supreme, I have failed my reality-existence. And I shall continue to fail my Beloved Supreme and my reality-existence if I go on loving the finite in myself. But if I start loving only the

Infinite in myself, then I shall not be compelled to see the face of frustration, the face of failure. I shall only fly in the sky with my Eternity's beloved friend, my soul-bird. I shall remain inside the Golden Boat of my Eternity's Pilot Supreme, sailing, sailing towards an unhorizoned Divinity-Land and Immortality-Shore.

My new life will be a life of life-transcending and God-inviting Smile. My old life gave me what it had: fear of God, fear of desire, fear in desire. My new life gives me the message of love of God and the fulfilment of God in God's own Way. I am preparing for God, to become His supremely chosen instrument, Him to love, Him to please, Him to fulfil always and always, in His own Way.

EA 45. *16 July 1977, 12:20 p.m. — John F Kennedy High School, Bronx, New York.*

46. HUMILITY AND COMPASSION

What I have is humility, and what God has is Compassion. Humility is my soulful gift to my Lord Supreme. Compassion is my Lord's fruitful gift to me.

My humility is supported by two significant members of my inner family: softness and tenderness. God's Compassion is supported by two sublime members of His inner family: Love and Concern.

My hidden treasure is my fully blossomed humility. God's open treasure is His fully revealed Compassion.

My humility has a free access not only to those who love me and need me, but also to those who do not love me and who do not need me. God's Compassion is always unconditional. God's Compassion is for all. It is the seeker in me, on the strength of his receptivity, who receives God's Compassion. God the Compassion is only for those who try and try, but for whom success still remains a far cry. Just because God the Compassion is for them, ultimately they will not only receive God the Compassion, but they will also become most perfect instruments of God.

I am my humility-tree to please my Lord Supreme in His own Way. God is His Compassion-rain to fulfil me and immortalise me in His own supreme Way.

EA 46. *16 July 1977, 6:25 p.m. — in transit to New Jersey.*

47. OBEDIENCE

I need obedience; I love obedience. I need my superior; I love my superior. My superior is my pathfinder. My superior is all responsibility. He liberates me from worry, anxiety, hesitation, fear and doubt. The uncomely forces that could easily have assailed me are well taken care of or, rather, are under the full control of my superior.

My obedience to my superior is not a forced surrender of mine. It is only my conscious awareness of superior divinity that is above me. But there shall come a time, through my continuous progress, when I shall be able to become one with my superior; I shall be on the same footing as my superior so that we can derive mutual joy. A real superior is he who cries and tries to bring up the inferior to his own standard so that he can play, sing and dance with him.

God is my only superior. Unless and until He can see me standing side by side with Him, His Manifestation-Light will not be able to permeate His entire creation. The human in me wants and needs a superior for protection and guidance. The divine in God wants and needs a partner, a collaborator, and not an inferior creation in order to be divinely cheerful and supremely fruitful.

EA 47. *16 July 1977, 6:45 p.m. — in transit to New Jersey.*

48. I NEED MORE

I need more. I need more peace. I need more joy. Peace I need in my mind. Joy I need in my heart.

I need more. I need more soulfulness. I need more selflessness. Soulfulness I need in my vital. Selflessness I need in my body.

I need more. I need more determination. I need more perfection. Determination I need in my aspiration. Perfection I need in my dedication.

I need more. I need more Compassion. I need more co-operation. Compassion I need from my Beloved Supreme in my very existence-reality. Co-operation I need from humanity in all that I do, all that I say and all that I grow into.

When I have more peace in my mind, more joy in my heart, more soulfulness in my vital, more selflessness in my body, more determination in my aspiration, more perfection in my dedication, more Compassion from God and more co-operation from humanity, at that time I shall become a most perfect instrument of God in the inner world and a most perfect representative of mankind in the outer world. I need more, I need more.

EA 48. *16 July 1977, 9:05 p.m. — Kean College, Union, New Jersey.*

49. SALVATION, LIBERATION, REALISATION, PERFECTION AND SATISFACTION

Are you a sinner? Then you definitely need salvation. Are you utterly earth-bound? Then you certainly need liberation. Are you helplessly isolated? Then you surely need realisation. Are you totally dissatisfied with your desire-life? Then you unmistakably need perfection. Are you ready to love God and serve God in God's own Way? Then you unquestionably need satisfaction.

Pray. Your salvation-problem will be over. Devote yourself to God. Your liberation-problem will be over. Meditate. Your realisation-problem will be over. Cry from within. Your perfection-problem will be over. Feel that you are only of God and only for God. Your satisfaction-problem will be over.

Salvation is in the Christ-world. Liberation is in the Buddha-world. Realisation is in the oneness-world. Perfection is in the Krishna-world. Satisfaction is only in the God-fulfilment-world.

EA 49. *16 July 1977, 10:00 p.m. — in transit to Jamaica, New York.*

50. CHARITY

Charity I do not like. I like concern, true concern. When someone shows me charity, I feel a sense of inferiority, and when I offer charity to someone, I undoubtedly feel a sense of superiority. I want neither a superior feeling nor an inferior feeling: what I want is an equal feeling.

The Christian world believes that charity means an open door to Heaven, but it is totally mistaken, utterly mistaken, hopelessly mistaken. Charity does not mark or determine a sense of true concern and true love, and when true concern and true love are wanting, the door of Heaven can never be open. It will always remain closed. It is not charity, but the feeling of oneness, that opens the door of Heaven. If there is no feeling of oneness, then no matter how much money-power, material wealth or anything I offer to someone, it is bound to take me to the ignorance-world where the dance of superiority and inferiority is going on.

When a part of my existence needs to receive or achieve something and another part comes to its rescue, their sense of oneness immediately opens the door of Heaven for me. If there is something beautiful, and if my mind immediately helps my eye to appreciate its beauty, then there is a oneness-feeling. If my mind wants to study something, and my legs carry me to the school or the library, then there is a oneness-feeling.

Charity cannot give me satisfaction. Charity cannot open the door of Heaven to me. It is only the feeling of oneness that can give me satisfaction, and this feeling of oneness has to be enlarged. When I give someone material wealth, money-power or something else, I have to feel that it is my very necessity to increase my own oneness-feeling for the length and breadth of the world. I have to feel that it is not I who am helping someone. It is I, on the contrary, who am being helped. This charity is not charity; far from it. It is my self-giving in order to realise my higher self totally, integrally, here in the world.

My oneness-offering not only opens the door of Heaven to me, but also opens the doors of Infinity, Eternity and Immortality, for oneness is God's first Vision-Song and His ultimate, ever-transcending Vision-Reality-Dance. If I want to sing God's Vision-Song, then my larger part and my smaller part have to be God's Reality-Dance in this endlessly ever-transcending Reality.

EA 50. *17 July 1977, 7:35 a.m. — Jamaica High School Track, Jamaica, New York.*

51. EXAMINATION

"My Beloved Lord Supreme, do tell me only one thing to satisfy my curiosity. Do You try to examine me? You say that You do not try to examine me, but it seems to me that at times You do try to examine me. Am I correct in my feeling?"

"My child, to be very frank with you, I do not examine you. Examination is not a way of teaching anybody. Examination only creates fear, undue fear, in the student, no matter how brilliant the student is. The student fears that he will fail and be embarrassed, and then the world will look down upon him. What you call examination, I call illumination-game. I do not examine you to pass you or fail you. I just want to play the illumination-game with you so that you do not underestimate your capacity or overestimate your capacity. When you underestimate your capacity, unconsciously you cherish false modesty, and when you overestimate your capacity, you make friends with an exorbitant depression-ignorance. To underestimate one's capacity and to overestimate one's capacity are equally bad.

"In your life of aspiration and dedication, when you play the game of illumination, you have to feel the necessity of bringing your inner cry to the fore, and also your ignorance-lethargy to the fore. You have to surrender not only the divine part of your existence but also the undivine part.

"So My examination is not an examination in the true sense of the term. It is an offering for your self-perfection. In your present state of consciousness, ignorance and light, falsehood and truth your mind has cleverly accumulated in your body-consciousness and vital consciousness. I wish you to offer to Me all that you have and all that you are. It is integral self-offering which you must make. You will get illumination from Me through the process of purification and self-offering of all that you have. What you have to offer is your beauty-heart. It is the beauty of your own existence within and without, that you offer. The lesser beauty, which you call ignorance, and the higher beauty you have to offer to Me, and in return I will offer you self-illumination.

"This is the game I play with you. It is our illumination-game and never, never, never an examination — far from it! It is a joint illumination."

EA 51. *17 July 1977, 8:40 a.m. — Jamaica High School Track, Jamaica, New York.*

52. GIFTS

"My Beloved Supreme, I have some gifts for You. My first gift is my soulful cry. My second gift is my fruitful smile. My third and special gift is my oneness-heart. My fourth and extra-special gift is my gratitude-flame."

"My child, I am all gratitude to you, and I have also a gift for you. This is My gift: I need you infinitely more than you can ever imagine. With you I started My Vision's journey; with you I shall reach My Reality's Satisfaction-Goal."

EA 52. *17 July 1977, 3:00 p.m. — in transit from Jamaica, New York to Washington, D.C..*

53. WHO IS THE WINNER?

Who is the winner? Not he who wins, but he who has established his cheerful oneness with the result, which is an experience in the form of failure or success, a journey forward or a journey backward.

Who is the winner? Not he who wins the race, but he who loves to run sleeplessly and breathlessly with God the supreme Runner.

Who is the winner? Not he whose glory we sing, but he who embodies God's Compassion-Light in abundant measure.

Who is the winner? Not he who has acquired tremendous name and fame and amassed a big fortune, but he who requires only one thing: God-satisfaction in God's own Way.

EA 53. *17 July 1977, 3:05 p.m. — in transit from Jamaica, New York to Washington, D.C..*

54. TWO TRAINS

Two trains: the train of desire and the train of aspiration. The desire-train starts at the nothingness-hunger-station and stops at the frustration-starvation-station. The aspiration-train starts at the soulfulness-thirst-station and stops at the illumination-feast-station.

If you are a passenger on the desire-train, you may not actually know what is good for you and what is bad for you. You will enter into the desire-train only to suffer. If you are a passenger on the aspiration-train, you do not have to know what is good and what is bad for you, for God Himself chooses for you. Therefore, once you enter into the aspiration-train, you will only prosper and prosper both in the inner world and in the outer world. The inner prosperity is your heart's breathless cry. The outer prosperity is your life's sleepless smile.

EA 54. *17 July 1977, 3:10 p.m. — in transit from Jamaica, New York to Washington, D.C..*

55. WHO IS KNOCKING?

Who is knocking? Satan? Do not bother me. Today I have many important things to do.

Who is knocking? Man? Please come at some other time. Unfortunately, I am quite busy now.

Who is knocking? God? Why do You embarrass me, Lord? Do You need my permission to enter into my heart-room?

"My son, perhaps you are not fully ready to receive Me. I am knocking just to inform you that I shall come again to visit your gratitude-room, your surrender-shrine and your perfection-self-offering. My son, you take your own time. I am not at all in a hurry. But I shall definitely come to pay you My blessingful Visit."

EA 55. *17 July 1977, 3:15 p.m. — in transit from Jamaica, New York to Washington, D.C..*

56. DISOBEDIENCE AND PENALTY

Disobedience and penalty: are they inseparable friends? Yes, they are. Our mother Eve disobeyed, and our father Adam disobeyed. They disobeyed once, only once, but they were forced to pay a severe penalty, and they did pay the penalty. Alas, what is worse, we who are their descendants are still paying the penalty, paying for their disobedience. Is it fair? Perhaps it is; perhaps it is not. In humanity's eye the penalty was, is and remains unbearable. In Divinity's Eye this penalty is more than negligible in comparison to the fathomless Love, Joy, Concern and Blessings that our parents, Eve and Adam, received from God before they descended, nay, before they helplessly and hopelessly fell from the Garden of Eden.

Our old family's old friend was sin; but at long last we have mustered courage, inner and outer, to have two new friends: a self-giving cry and a God-becoming smile.

EA 56. *17 July 1977, 3:20 p.m. — in transit from Jamaica, New York to Washington, D.C..*

57. SECRETS

God's secret is a beginningless Silence. Man's secret is an endless sound.

God's secret is to give what He has: Compassion. Man's secret is to possess from others what he does not have: material wealth, power and other things.

God's secret is to create and divinely enjoy a new Vision-Light. Man's secret is to destroy everything that he sees, to destroy everyone that he knows.

God's secret is to forgive and forget constantly. Man's secret is never to forgive, never to forget.

God's secret is to cry soulfully before He smiles satisfactorily. Man's secret is to cry before he dies and cry while he is dying so that he can reach God's Heaven and be greeted by God Himself. At this, God does not know whether to smile or cry. Therefore, He laughs.

EA 57. *17 July 1977, 3:25 p.m. — in transit from Jamaica, New York to Washington, D.C..*

58. SOMETHING IS MISSING

Something is missing. What is it? Man's gratitude-drop. Something is found. What is it? Man's haughty pride. Who needs it? Nobody! No, not even the all-devouring death.

Something is missing. What is it? Man's service-hands. Something is found. What is it? Man's feeling of worthlessness. Who needs it? Nobody! No, not even the worst possible fool on earth.

Something is missing. What is it? Man's responsibility-tree. Something is found. What is it? Man's satisfaction-compromise. Who needs it? Nobody! No, not even the saint who is all forgiveness. The saint is willing to forgive ignorance, but he will never make any compromise with ignorance-illusion.

EA 58. *17 July 1977, 9:10 p.m. — American University, Washington D.C..*

59. OFF THE PATH

You are off the path. What does it mean? Does it mean that from now on you will be helpless, hopeless and useless? No, far from it. From now on only one thing will happen and that is the fulfilment of your oneness with your vital and your vital life. Your vital has chalked out a path for you and you want to walk along that path. Previously, you were walking along the path of the soul. There the soul was your leader-friend. Now your vital will be your leader-friend.

When you walked on your soul's path, you made many promises to God, inner promises. These promises, from now on, you will be under no obligation to fulfil. God, too, made a solemn promise to you, and His promise that He would grant you conscious liberation from the meshes of ignorance, and absolute oneness with Him, is also withdrawn. You can say temporarily, you can say indefinitely; it depends on how long your friendship with your vital leader-friend lasts.

Now you have left the path of the soul and you have entered into the path of the vital. If you criticise the path of the soul, if you feel that there is nothing worthwhile to be found on the path of the soul, and that it was a terrible mistake on your part to enter into that path, then naturally you will stay indefinitely on the vital path.

Now you have decided that the path of the vital is the true path, the path where you will succeed, where you will meet with satisfaction. If this is what you feel, then not only are you mistaken, but the real in you, the soul in you, will not put up with such an absurd statement. Your soul will indefinitely withdraw. But if you feel that the path of the soul was hard, arduous and difficult for you, and if you have chosen this other path because it is a lesser path, an easier path, then your soul will forgive you and wait for you with absolute patience. The soul feels that your helplessness and hopelessness is not a thing to be encouraged or justified; far from it. But the compassion of the soul will rain on your weakness, and the soul will grant you another chance in two years or five years or ten years. But if you find fault with the soul's discrimination, if you criticise the soul's attempt to execute God's Will in and through you, then the soul will withdraw from you for quite a few years or for this entire incarnation. It may happen that this withdrawal may even last for quite a few incarnations — if you believe in reincarnation, of course.

When you go off the path, it is parting time between you and your soul. When you become one with your vital-friend, your soul will withdraw. When you leave the path, you are saying goodbye. You tell the soul, "Someday in the distant future our ways shall cross." The soul soulfully says, "I hope so."

EA 59. *18 July 1977, 6:45 a.m. — Jamaica High School track, Jamaica, New York.*

60. DISOBEDIENCE IS THE ORDER OF THE DAY

Disobedience is the order of the day. No matter what I do, no matter how many times I write about disobedience, no matter how many times I speak about disobedience, it seems that disobedience from the disciples will never end. Even yesterday I spoke about disobedience, about what happened when Adam and Eve disobeyed God. Then later, when we were on the bus, I asked you people to sing. There was not even one enthusiastic singer. I blame the leader of your group one hundred per cent. If the leader does not have the necessary obedience and enthusiasm, then it is a really painful shock. I won't blame anybody else if you go to sleep or do not show interest. But from the leader if there is no enthusiastic movement or approach to the rest of the members, then I feel very sad. And from the members also there should have been two or three to come and inspire the leader to sing. Now, I am the supreme leader. When I say, "Do something," if the disciples don't agree, or go to sleep, then I will take care of them in my own way. But the leader that I appoint also has to be responsible.

On the one hand I am taking you people here, there, elsewhere. You don't get time to practise and I am sorry. But again, I feel that these things are absolutely necessary to spread my light. Yesterday quite a few people came to our concert. They were extremely receptive. In the bus you had plenty of time to practise, but whatever pleases you, you do. What pleases me, you had no time to do. For one hour or so you entered into the entertainment-world. That is what you did.

When I take your time away and you cannot practise, I compensate. But when I ask you to sing, at that time you are tired, unwilling, exhausted. You may think that this is nothing; Guru will not take it seriously. But I will take it seriously even if I ask you to budge an inch and do not give any rhyme or reason. If you do not do it, then it is recorded on the tablet of my heart. You don't think that I am asking you to do something important; I am not asking you to jump off the Empire State Building to show the world that you are obedient. To do something striking in order to show your obedience is easy. But real obedience has to take place at every moment, in every action. If I request that you move an inch, please feel that this request is of paramount importance. It is as if I have asked you for everything. The mind will say, "This is easier than the easiest. Therefore, if I don't do it, no harm." But if you do not do something extremely easy, will you do something very difficult?

From now on I want you people to take any request from me as a divine command. I have had enough sad experiences. Even when I ask you to do something in a light vein, you have to do it. From now on, no matter who the disciple is, if I make a mere request, do it. Otherwise, your disobedience in the inner world will be digging your own grave. From now on, please take my request as a divine command, coming consciously from the Absolute Supreme. Otherwise, I will be very sad and disturbed. For yesterday's disobedience I blame your leader one hundred per cent. I won't blame others, because the leader is my representative in a specific field. I don't know what I shall do with you people in the future if I see disobedience reigning supreme in your lives. So please, please, do not disobey me.

You do not know who I am. Unfortunately or fortunately, I know who I am. If I know who I am to you, to God, to the entire world, I have to behave to you in that way. If you are prepared to sing with me and dance with me, then when I say, "Sit down," you have to do it. This kind of obedience you need.

This applies to all of you. I show you tremendous love, affection, concern, everything. Even your stupid mind will sometimes believe it. The other day I gave a talk on how I will use my Justice-Height, and not my Compassion-Light. I ask you in this life to do or not to do only one or two things. When I ask you two, three, four times not to do something, afterwards I will become very strict. I will give you a last warning, and if you still disobey me, then I will ask you to leave the Centre. It is very, very painful for me to ask people who have been with us for many years to leave. But only for one reason do I ask people to leave the Centre, and that is disobedience. I will accept or tolerate almost anything that you do except disobedience, because disobedience is just like standing against me. There are two armies fighting. When you openly disobey me, you go to the enemy's side and fight against the Supreme, against the Supreme's Will.

Please, please, I beg of you, never disobey me, especially when it is a matter of your emotional life and vital life, which is your immediate destruction. If you disobey me in any aspect of life, at that time I forgive you, but when it is emotional life, I ask you not to do it, especially on the outer plane. On the inner plane you may say that you didn't get the message. But on the outer plane once I tell you, then you can't deny it later on.

So to all of you I am saying: please, please do not disobey me. If you disobey me, you are revolting against the Will of the Supreme in me. If you stay outside the Centre, you can enjoy yourself and do whatever you like. But when there is a rebellion inside our sweet little family, I will not be able to put up with it. I have asked two disciples to leave the Centre. My heart breaks, but I abide by the Will of the Supreme. I have no other means to deal with those people. Tomorrow may be your turn if you disobey me. I have to be very strict with you people on the basis of my own oneness with the Supreme. Then there is no father, no mother, no brother, no sister, no son. If I ask you to do something and you don't do it, then the same kind of fate will befall you tomorrow.

One aspect of mine is singing and dancing with you people. I am your constant friend, your eternal friend. Again, I may have to ask you to leave the Centre, to leave our sweet little family, so that you will not have any conflict between your spiritual life and your outer life. If I have given a warning to any of you here, please take it as the last warning. Then, if you go on disobeying, you know what will be your fate. So be careful, be careful, be careful. If you do the right thing, you are absolutely a jewel inside my gratitude-heart. But if you disobey me, your disobedience will take you people far, far, far away from me. Then you will be totally lost — totally! — and my presence will be sadly missing from your lives.

EA 60. *18 July 1977, 6:55 a.m. — Jamaica High School track, Jamaica, New York.*

61. THE RED STOPLIGHT

The red stoplight discourages me when I am in a hurry. The same red light soothes my life when I am not in a hurry.

I want to enjoy the life-breath of time. The red stoplight tells me that life is not always a smooth passage. It warns me for my own good. In no way does it try to prevent me from manifesting my life-saving speed and my life-saving reality.

The red stoplight is my true friend in disguise. In the spiritual world, the red light is my conscience. My conscience never prevents me from doing the right thing; it only wants me not to do undivine things. It is always eager to warn me against doing the wrong thing, and to inspire me to do the right thing.

When I don't obey the red stoplight, I enter into alarming danger, into the very jaws of death. Similarly, when I don't listen to the soft, sweet, smiling dictates of my conscience, I may run into dire catastrophe in my life of aspiration. My conscience does not discourage me or prevent me from doing the right thing, but it asks me to remain cautious so that the hungry tiger of the animal-human world does not destroy me.

Because of my conscience, I am a human being. If I abide by the soulful dictates of my conscience, I shall see only the face of satisfaction in my life. This satisfaction is the very beginning of my blossoming belief. When I am satisfied, I blossom forth. When I blossom forth, I feel that I am not only an instrument but *the* instrument of my Beloved Supreme.

I forever love you and adore you, red stoplight! You are truly the saviour of my outer life. O my conscience, I love and adore you because you are truly the saviour of my inner life. Because of you, I do not dine with ignorance-night; I am safely driving towards Eternity's Light, Infinity's Beauty and Immortality's Love.

EA 61. *18 July 1977, 8:15 a.m. — Jamaica High School track, Jamaica, New York.*

62. YESTERDAY WAS THE TIME

Yesterday was the time for me to sympathise with the suffering humanity. Today is the time for me to express my genuine concern for the bewildered humanity. Tomorrow will be the time for me to offer my loving service to the desiring humanity. But now, now is the time for me to express my oneness-heart with the hungry humanity.

Sympathy, concern, service, oneness-heart: these are the real members of my inmost family, and these members of my inmost family I wish to share with the rest of the world, with God's creation, with God the creation.

EA 62. *18 July 1977, 12:30 p.m. — Sri Chinmoy Centre, Jamaica, New York.*

63. TO BE DIVINELY GREAT

To be divinely great is to serve. To be supremely good is to love. To be eternally perfect is to cry within sleeplessly. To be satisfied in God's own Way is to become consciously and constantly a heart of gratitude-flood.

The human in me desires greatness. The divine in me longs for goodness. The aspiring and ascending God within me yearns for perfection. The loving and manifesting God in me cries for satisfaction.

I wish to become a most intimate and lifelong friend of greatness, goodness, perfection and satisfaction, for it is through them that my Beloved Supreme will smile His eternal Smile and dance His immortal Dance in and for me. May our friendship not only please the human and divine within us, but also please and fulfil our Beloved Supreme deep within us.

EA 63. *18 July 1977, 12:35 p.m. — Sri Chinmoy Centre, Jamaica, New York.*

64. IF YOU WANT TO BE GREAT

If you want to be great, then keep yourself busy learning everything — everything in everything and everything of everything.

If you want to be good, then keep yourself busy unlearning the things you have learnt in the desire-world, and keep yourself busy learning everything in the aspiration-world.

If you want to be only in the realisation-world, and not in the desire-world or in the aspiration-world, then you do not have to learn anything and you do not have to unlearn anything. You have only to become what you want to become. How can you become what you want to become? You can easily become what you want to become only when you feel that you can never make yourself what you want to become. No human power can do it. Only by the Grace that comes from Above can you do what you want to do and become what you want to become.

How do you get this Grace? You get this Grace if at every moment you shed loving tears of gratitude to the Supreme for what He has done for you out of His infinite Bounty and, again, for what, out of His infinite Bounty, He has not done for you. Many things God has given you out of His infinite Bounty, so that you can be happy, the divine in you can be happy. Again, many things He has not given you for your good. So, because of what He has given you and what He has not given you, you must create a sense of continuous gratitude. Inside that gratitude you are bound to see Him, feel Him and become one with Him in His Divinity's integral Life.

EA 64. *18 July 1977, 12:40 p.m. — Sri Chinmoy Centre, Jamaica, New York.*

65. GRATITUDE

We are grateful to God, for He is with us here and now. We are grateful to God, for He has created within us a genuine hunger for Him. We are grateful to God, for He has given us a long express train of hope. We are grateful to God, for He has repeatedly told us that He will keep His promise. What is His promise? His promise is that He will not be satisfied unless and until each creation of His satisfies Him in His own Way.

How can we please God in His own Way? First of all, we are now aware of God's Way of operating. Also, we may feel that something will please God, but how can we know if we are correct in our feelings, or whether it is all mental hallucination? There is a way to know whether we are pleasing God in God's own Way. We have to dive deep within and destroy or transform the thought-world and replace it with will-power, adamantine will-power. If we are afraid of God's Will-Power, which is all-powerful, then our life will always remain in untold fear.

We are on earth, here and now, only to please God in God's own Way. It is a difficult task indeed, but we get joy only when we cross hurdles. If we do not cross hurdles, then there will be no lasting reality and there will be no lasting satisfaction. If we do not do everything here and now, then there will be no satisfaction whatsoever, for today's goal is only the beginning of tomorrow's new journey. This new journey and the journey's goal will come and greet us, for the achievements of the soul and the journey's goal are inseparable.

When we cry with gratitude, it is the journey's soul that acts in and through us, which is a splendid achievement. And when we smile with gratitude, it is the journey's goal that has become one with aspiration's starting point and with aspiration's ever-transcending horizon.

EA 65. *18 July 1977, 12:45 p.m. — Sri Chinmoy Centre, Jamaica, New York.*

66. IN THE HUMAN WORLD

In the human world there are three things that last forever. At least, so do I think. These are: fear, one's sense of unworthiness and a doubting and suspicious mind.

In the divine world there are three things that will undoubtedly forever last. These are: faith, courage and love. If a disciple has these three things, then he does not need anything else.

Fear, anxiety and doubt: these are immortal, but in a negative, destructive way, whereas faith, courage and love represent or embody Immortality in a positive way. The human in us will one day transcend itself and accept the divine in us with all its faith, courage and love.

EA 66. *18 July 1977, 7:00 p.m. — in transit to Connecticut Sri Chinmoy Centre.*

67. OUR BELOVED SUPREME

Our Beloved Supreme is always ready to lead us, but it is we who have to cultivate the desire to follow Him. Our Beloved Supreme is always eager, more than eager, to make us feel that He loves us constantly, but it is we who have to cultivate the willingness to believe Him.

Our Beloved Supreme is always ready to help us fight against ignorance-night, but it is we who have to feel the real necessity to be in wisdom-light and not in ignorance-night. If we want wisdom-light, then only shall we accept His Service.

Our Beloved Supreme is always ready and more than eager to cry for us to attain the highest Reality-Height, but He expects in return just a little soulful smile from us. If we do not offer Him a little soulful smile, then He will not be able to create a receptivity-vessel within us. If we do not have a receptacle within us, then when He cries for us, we will not be able to see Him crying or feel His cry. So what we need is a receptivity-vessel when He cries. This receptivity-vessel is nothing short of an echo-reality, for His cry has to echo and re-echo in the inmost recesses of our hearts. This is what our Beloved Supreme longs for from us, so that He can cry and cry from His own ever-transcending Heights only for our salvation, liberation, realisation and perfection — for us, only for us.

EA 67. *18 July 1977, 7:05 p.m. — in transit to Connecticut Sri Chinmoy Centre.*

68. GOD'S COMPASSION FLOWS, GOD'S JUSTICE GROWS

God's Compassion tells me that I can do nothing without Him. God's Justice tells me that He has given me the necessary capacity to become what I sincerely, soulfully want to become. Not only will God's Justice give me what I divinely want to have, but also it will give me the capacity to become as perfect as God Himself.

The hero in us cries for God's Justice. The beggar in us cries for God's Compassion. The hero in us knows perfectly well that when God exercises His Justice, the hero will be able to run faster than the fastest and will eventually become wiser than the wisest. On him God will shower His better-than-the-best Concern-Height and Love-Delight. Again, in order to make us great, good and divine, God the Compassion is constantly showering His Compassion on us.

The beggar in us is also laziness incarnate. He begs, but only for a short while; then he gives up totally. He does not have the necessary capacity to stick to his principles and be ready to pay the price. The beggar in us only wants Compassion unconditionally from God. God can give His unconditional Concern and Love to the beggar in us, but once we get it, then there is every possibility that the beggar in us will not appreciate it because it was given unconditionally. When God does something unconditionally and man does not do anything to deserve it, then man does not value it. Therefore, God always expects us to do something — to try, to cry — in order to value His Gifts. God can give us whatever we want, whatever we need, but it is we who will not be satisfied. It is we who will not be pleased with ourselves unless we have offered our mite to God's Cosmic Plan.

God fervently wishes that the beggar in us will one day give up begging and start choosing like a divine hero, a supreme hero, who knows what he wants and, in order to get it, offers up his body, vital, mind, heart and soul as a flaming sacrifice. We must not remain always veritable beggars. It is high time for us, it is our bounden duty, to grow into divine heroes and live the life of supreme heroism. What is the supreme heroism? The supreme heroism is to give ourselves ceaselessly and unconditionally so that God can fulfil Himself in and through us in His own Way. When He fulfils Himself in His own Way, it means that He is liberating, fulfilling and immortalising His expanded and extended Cosmic Reality.

EA 68. *18 July 1977, 7:10 p.m. — in transit to Connecticut Sri Chinmoy Centre.*

69. TO LIVE IN THE DESIRE-WORLD

To live in the desire-world is to live on tiptoe. How long can one live on tiptoe where anxiety, worry, tension, fear and doubt reign supreme? In the desire-world, the poison of the individual and the poison of the world, in secrecy supreme, kill each other. The world is killed by the individual's poison and the world kills the individual with its poison. This poison comes into existence from jealousy, doubt and suspicion.

The only way one can stop living on tiptoe is to feel that one is God's creation. The creation can never be neglected by the Creator. As ordinary human beings we do not destroy even a little painting that we have done. So how can God the Creator, whose creation is nothing but an exact image of His own Reality-Existence, destroy the world? Each individual has to feel that it is the need of the Supreme to create him, it is the need of the Supreme to sustain him, it is the need of the Supreme to fulfil him in a divine way.

To live on tiptoe is to forget one's Source, who is also the Source of Light and Delight. To live on tiptoe is to consciously make friends with the negative, destructive world, the temptation-world, where worry, anxiety, fear and doubt run riot.

Instead of living on tiptoe, you can live in the very heart of the Lord's divine Pride, provided you feel that it is your own duty, your sole duty, to cast aside your personal necessity and become one with your Beloved Supreme's divine Necessity. Your own necessity is desire-bound, and when it is fulfilled, inside it destruction looms large. So if you want to find your true satisfaction, then find it at the right place: inside God's

Compassion-Height. That is the only place to discover your satisfaction-right.

You are following the path of spirituality. Your heart is all aspiration. In the life of aspiration you are preparing for a life of total surrender. You will not only surrender your aspiration-life and dedication-life, but also your desire-life, your ignorance-life, with equal joy, equal love, equal confidence, equal certainty. Only then will there be no necessity on your part to hide from God or to try to hide your thoughts from Him. You and your integral existence must always reside in the Supreme. This is the only way for you to become totally perfect and inseparably one with Eternity's Vision-Light and Infinity's Manifestation-Delight.

EA 69. *18 July 1977, 7:15 p.m. — in transit to Connecticut Sri Chinmoy Centre.*

70. I WAS A STUDENT OF PRAYER

I was a student of prayer, but I can't say that I enjoyed my studies. When I was a student of prayer, anxiety and worry killed me. At times even fear and doubt killed me.

Then I became a student of meditation. When I was a student of meditation, at times I had confidence in my meditation, and at times I totally lacked confidence. Therefore, I did not succeed in a striking manner. Because meditation is all peace-expansion, light-expansion, love-expansion and oneness-expansion, I could have progressed fast, very fast. But I did not.

When I became a student of self-giving, I discovered immediately that my self-giving was growing into something infinitely more than I had ever dreamed of, something that I never would have had the capacity to acquire. What was it? A fruitful life of God-becoming vision-light and God-manifesting manifestation-delight.

I want to remain only a student of self-giving. The other two I do not want, I do not need separately. I do not need them as a separate existence in my self-giving. My self-giving includes meditation, prayer, everything. Therefore, what I need always is a self-giving cry and a self-giving smile.

EA 70. *18 July 1977, 7:20 p.m. — in transit to Connecticut Sri Chinmoy Centre.*

71. I WANTED TO TELL GOD

I wanted to tell God that I sincerely love Him. It was on the tip of my tongue. Alas, Satan came. As soon as I saw Satan, I totally forgot to tell God what I had intended to say.

I wanted to tell God that I need Him constantly. It was on the tip of my tongue. Alas, alas, Satan came at that very moment and ruined my inspiration. The very presence of Satan ruined all my joy, and I totally forgot to tell God what I had intended to say.

I wanted to tell God that I shall become unconditionally His most devoted instrument. It was all planned. It was on the tip of my tongue. Alas, Satan came and gave me an unwarranted frown. His frown took away all my inspiration, all my joy. All at once I felt miserable, and I enjoyed my misery to such an extent that I totally forgot to tell my Beloved Supreme what I had intended to say.

I wanted to tell my ignorance-friend that I would no longer speak to him. I had it all planned. It was on the tip of my tongue. Ah, who came to strengthen my promise? My Beloved Supreme.

I wanted to tell ignorance that from now on mine is the way of light, mine is the goal of delight, and that I must leave ignorance for good. It was on the tip of my tongue. Ah, who came to strengthen my promise? My eternally old, everlastingly old and, at the same time, ever-amazingly new friend, my Beloved Supreme.

EA 71. *18 July 1977, 7:25 p.m. — in transit to Connecticut Sri Chinmoy Centre.*

72. I LIVED ONLY TWICE

I lived only twice: once in the kingdom of strangling and devouring animals and once in the kingdom of doubting and suspecting human beings.

I am living now only twice: once in the world of hesitation and once in the world of unawareness.

I shall be living only twice: once in the smile of my gratitude-heart and once in the heart of God's Satisfaction-Light.

To grow and experience more and more, to become most spiritually mature, I shall live only twice: once inside the aspiration-plant and once inside the realisation-tree and realisation-fruit.

From now on, I shall make it a special point to live in my aspiration-world. There I shall see that my beloved Lord is crying and ascending to open up a new world of light, a new world of promise.

EA 72. *18 July 1977, 7:30 p.m. — in transit to Connecticut Sri Chinmoy Centre.*

73. I SHALL SING TODAY

I shall sing today. I shall sing the song of God's Beauty within me, in my inner world. I shall sing the song of God's Duty without me, in my outer world.

I shall sing today not the song which I knew so well, the song of frustration, but I shall sing a new song, the song of illumination.

I shall sing today only of the awakening, only of the manifesting divinity of my Beloved Supreme; I will never, never sing the song of self-unfoldment.

I shall sing today the song of perfection in the aspiring finite life.

I shall sing today the song of the Supreme, my Supreme Pilot, inside the cry of the finite.

I shall sing today, for this is the only way I can not only expedite my life's journey but also bring my goal slowly, steadily and unerringly closer to my reality-existence.

I shall sing today the song that I just learnt from my Beloved Supreme, and this song is the song of continuous self-offering. What is self-offering? Self-offering is the discovery of one's God-embracing reality.

EA 73. *18 July 1977, 7:35 p.m. — in transit to Connecticut Sri Chinmoy Centre.*

74. THE PURPOSE OF HUMAN LIFE

The purpose of the animal life is the quest for individuality and separativity. The purpose of human life is the quest for unity, and not a sense of separativity. The purpose of divine life is the quest for perfection — perfection in the inner world, perfection in the outer world, perfection in God's entire creation. The purpose of the Supreme's Life is the quest for satisfaction, the satisfaction that nourishes the body-reality of His creation and the soul-reality of His ever-transcending Vision.

Animal life is always hurtful. Human life is always doubtful. Divine life is always soulful. The Supreme's Life is always fruitful.

The animal life tells me that by fighting I will get everything. The human life tells me that by becoming clever I can get everything. The divine life tells me that by giving everything I shall become everything that I want to become and, something more, that I shall please God in His own Way. The Supreme's Life tells me that by oneness-spreading I shall not only become everything, but I shall be able to offer my all-becoming gift as a boon to the aspiring mankind.

EA 74. *18 July 1977, 7:40 p.m. — in transit to Connecticut Sri Chinmoy Centre.*

75. WHAT MORE CAN I GIVE YOU?

"My Lord Supreme, what more can I give You? I have given You my desire-day. I have given You my frustration-night. My Lord Supreme, what more can I give You? I have given You my anxiety-chain. I have given You my insecurity-train. What more can I give You, my Lord Supreme?

"My Lord Supreme, I have given You what I have learnt from my earthbound mind. I have given You what I have done, together with my hungry and aggressive vital. My Lord Supreme, what more can I give You? I have given You my hope-sky. I have given You my promise-sun. My Lord Supreme, what more can I give You, what more?"

"My child, I do not deny that you have given Me all these things that you have mentioned. But you have not given Me the thing that I need constantly from you so that I can be totally pleased and fulfilled, and that thing is your soul's satisfaction-breath. This is the only thing that I need from you. The rest of the things that you have given Me have brought Me joy, and I will do the needful with them. I shall transform them and make them into divine instruments of Mine. But the thing that I need constantly from you, the thing that I need most, you have not given Me so far. Therefore, I am reminding you to give Me your heart's oneness-cry, your soul's satisfaction-breath."

"O my sweet Father, O my dear Friend, O my only Boatman who is carrying me along Eternity's river towards Infinity's shore! They say that I am old, for I am over forty. They say that I am cold, that I have become a finished product, that I have long ago lost my childlike life, my nature's cry and smile. Is it all true?"

"No, no, no, My child. This is far, far from the truth. You are not old; you are bold. You are not cold; you are warm. You are not old, for in you and through you I have created a new world of self-revelation and self-manifestation to see and enjoy Me in the divine, Supreme way. This way is through art. You are not old. After you crossed the barrier of forty I made you a divinely, supremely chosen instrument of Mine and entered into you to reveal and manifest Myself in the world of painting and the world of music. Two giant worlds I have created in and through you for My own Satisfaction.

"You are not cold, you are warm. Because of your warmth, because of your oneness-warmth, humanity's ascending cry and divinity's descending smile have accepted you as My instrument, My most pleasing and fulfilling instrument.

"No matter how old you are according to the earthly calendar, you are not old; you can never be old, and all those who have become inseparably one with you also can never be old. Your oneness-friends, like you, will never be old in My Vision-Light, for you are all in My Golden Boat. My own Aspiration-Cry in and through you all is being manifested at My own choice Hour. My Aspiration-Cry is glowing and growing and offering haven to countless seekers of Truth and lovers of Light and Delight.

"You are not old, and all those over forty who are with you, in you and for you are like your four-year-old children, for they have the same warmth, the same eagerness to be in My Boat. Their eagerness and warmth they have offered to Me to be in My Boat. Therefore, they can never, never be old. They have given Me a free access to dream in and through them, and I am dreaming in and through them. When I dream in and through anybody, that person can never be old, for My

Dream is manifesting as an illumining, fulfilling reality that is eternally new, eternally illumining, eternally fulfilling.

"A life of dream, divine dream, is always a life of blossoming, becoming and transcending. All of you in the Golden Boat who are over forty, I am dreaming in and through you. Each one has a special dream. This Dream of Mine in each seeker-lover is My Life-Breath of new creation, new perfection, new satisfaction."

EA 75. *18 July 1977, 8:00 p.m. — Sri Chinmoy Centre, Norwalk, Connecticut.*

76. DIVINE PILGRIMAGE

Pilgrimage, my Divine pilgrimage.

My Beloved Lord, My Beloved Friend, My Beloved All. You have given me my simplicity. You have given me my sincerity. You have given me my serenity. You have given me my purity.

Simplicity You have given me so that I can start my pilgrimage along the road of my body-consciousness. Sincerity You have given me so that I can march along the road of my vital-dynamism. Serenity You have given me so that I can start my pilgrimage along the road of my mental vision. Purity You have given me so that I can start my pilgrimage along the road of my heart's delight.

My Lord Supreme, You have also told me that my simplicity, sincerity, serenity and purity will reach their acme of perfection only when my heart's gratitude flowers petal by petal, blossoming to perfect perfection. And for that what I need is constant self-giving — conscious, soulful and unconditional self-giving. In order to have conscious, constant and unconditional self-giving, what I need is a real approach to You — not as a beggar but as a lover; not as a beggar-destitute but as a lover-friend. If I approach You as a beggar, You will give me what I need or what I want. But my receptivity-vessel is so small that even if You give me what I need, it will not be much, it will be far from my full satisfaction. And if You give me what I want, it may not be the right thing. You will give me, but what You give me will ultimately be a source of true frustration and never a source of satisfaction.

My Lord Supreme, even if You give me an iota of what You want to give me, that very iota will not only please the real in me, the soul, but immortalise the human in me. The human in me is my human hope, my earthly hope. Hope before it bears fruit is nothing short of illusion and delusion – mental hallucination, to say the least. But even this very hope You will be able to immortalise. Once my hope is immortalised, I shall see my hope in the form of Your own Reality's Vision, transcendental Vision, and Your own Vision's Reality, universal Reality.

EA 76. *18 July 1977, 8:10 p.m. — Sri Chinmoy Centre, Norwalk, Connecticut.*

77. LORD OF MY LIFE, FRIEND OF MY HEART

O sweet beloved Lord of my life, O great and good Friend of my heart, I know, I know that to love You is to be found doing something for You. Since I am not to be found doing something for You, that means I do not truly love You.

O beloved Lord Supreme, I know, I know to serve You is to be found doing something for You. Alas, alas, since I am not found doing something for you, that means that I am not serving You.

O sweet Lord, I know, I know to think of You, to meditate on You, is to be found doing something for You. Alas, alas, since I am not found doing something for You, that means I do not think of You, I do not meditate on You.

O sweet Lord, to tell my inner world that I need You is to be found doing something for You, to tell the outer world that it needs You desperately, as I need You, is to be found doing something for You as God the creation. But alas, since I am found neither in the inner world doing something for You, nor in the outer world doing something for You, that means I do not need You; I am bound only to please myself in my own way.

But my soul's solemn promise was to please You and fulfil You in Your Way. To please You and fulfil You in Your own Way is not always to remain in the world of theory but to become practicality itself — the practicality of the reality that You want and need. It is in my practicality that You can manifest what You have for me, for humanity, and what You are to me and to humanity. What You have is Your inner creation Light for me and for the entire humanity; and what You are is a conscious, constant and inseparable oneness-cry in the inner world and oneness-smile in the outer world for me and for humanity.

EA 77. *18 July 1977, 8:20 p.m. — Sri Chinmoy Centre, Norwalk, Connecticut.*

78. ACCEPTANCE

I have accepted man
Because
Man is dreaming.

I have accepted the earth
Because
The earth is transcending.

I have accepted Heaven
Because
Heaven is smiling.

I have accepted the cosmic gods
Because
The cosmic gods are promising.

I have accepted God
Because
God is at once evolving and fulfilling.

I have accepted myself
Because
I am learning the supreme art
of surrendering.

EA 78. *19 July 1977, 7:30 a.m. — Jamaica High School Track, Jamaica, New York.*

79. EMPTY MOMENTS

You are saying that you suffer from empty moments. Do you know why? Not because you have nothing to do. Not because you have nothing to talk about. Not because you have nothing to read or write. Not because your world is wanting in friends. Not because you cannot trust the world. Not because you cannot claim anybody to be your own in this vast creation of God's. No, the reason you suffer from empty moments is because you are not playing inside the garden of your heart with your heart's child, the soul.

If you play lovingly, cheerfully, devotedly and unreservedly with your soul-child, then you will never, never suffer from empty moments no matter what the world gives you, no matter what the world does to you, no matter what you are doing and what you will be doing for this world of yours.

You are bound to suffer from empty moments. The empty moments will assail you unless and until you do the right thing, the only thing, which is your constant oneness-sport with your heart's child, the soul. Something more: you have to realise the supreme fact that a tiny, soulful smile by your soul is the saviour of your life, the liberator of your life and the fulfiller of your life. If you can catch the soul smiling, you are bound to make progress in your inner life and you are bound to succeed in your outer life. And when you smile simultaneously with the soul, you become what you eternally are in the inner world: God's own Satisfaction-Smile. Not empty moments, but a fulfilled and fulfilling smile is the only purpose of your existence-reality here on earth.

EA 79. *19 July 1977, 7:40 a.m. — Jamaica High School Track, Jamaica, New York.*

80. DO YOU WANT TO BE PERFECT?

Do you want to be perfect in every possible way? Then let Me ask you a few simple but life-illumining questions. Is your mind receptive to a small change? If so, then ask your mind not to be so doubtful and suspicious all the time. Is your vital receptive to a small change? If so, then ask your vital not to lord it over the world and to crush the world under its heavy weight. Is your body receptive to a small change? If so, then ask your body not to sleep shamelessly for so many hours at a stretch. Is your heart receptive to a small change? If so, then ask your heart not to be so helplessly and hopelessly timid.

One more question you will ask each of the members of your inner family. Is your mind receptive to a small change? If so, then ask your mind to empty itself of all its contents early in the morning so that I can enter into it and enjoy My Satisfaction-Rest at least for seven fleeting seconds. Is your vital receptive to a small change? If so, then ask your vital to spread its concern-wings all over the world. Then what shall I do? Do you know? With enormous pride I shall play with all-loving Concern-Wings with your vital. Is your body receptive to a small change? If so, then ask your body to wake up and look around and discover Me. I am hiding. If the body can trace Me, then I shall be more than willing to play with the body my hide-and-seek game, which even the cosmic gods most soulfully enjoy. Is your heart receptive to a small change? If so, then ask your heart to breathe in only the purity-breath and nothing else. Tell your heart that the purity-breath is the only thing that I live on. When I eat anything else, I suffer from stomach upset and from all kinds of ailments. It is only your heart's purity-breath that nourishes Me, sustains Me and gives Me the Nectar-Delight and Immortality-Strength to continue My cosmic Game, My cosmic Dance and My cosmic Oneness-Satisfaction.

EA 80. *19 July 1977, 7:45 a.m. — Jamaica High School Track, Jamaica, New York.*

81. WHERE ARE THEY?

Where is the ignorance-king? He is at work. Where is the desire-man? He is at work. Where is the Compassion-God? He is at work.

The ignorance-king, the desire-man and the Compassion-God want me to be their witness. If you want to know how they work, I am more than willing to tell you. The ignorance-king works untiringly. The desire-man works unconsciously. The Compassion-God works unconditionally.

The ignorance-king wants to devour the world. The desire-man wants to possess the world. The Compassion-God wants to illumine the world.

The ignorance-king says, "I do not want to love anything. I do not want to love anybody, but I want to be loved by the desire-man and by the Compassion-God."

The desire-man says, "I want to love the temptation of the ignorance-king and I want to love the forgiveness of the Compassion-God."

The Compassion-God says, "I want to love My own awakening evolution in the ignorance-king. I want to love My own aspiring evolution in the desire-man. I want to love My own all-transcending and all-illumining evolution in My own Dream-Boat and Reality-Shore."

EA 81. *19 July 1977, 10:15 p.m. — Co-op City, Bronx, New York.*

82. IT IS NEVER TOO LATE

It is never too late for me to become a good instrument of God.

It is never too late for me to pray to God and to meditate on God in the small hours of the morning.

It is never too late for me to serve my Beloved Supreme inside my brothers and sisters — mankind.

It is never too late for me to love my sisters and brothers — humanity — inside my Beloved Supreme.

It is never too late for me to tell my sweet Lord that I am only for Him. Him to see face to face, Him to love, serve and fulfil, for this I saw the light of day.

It is never too late for me to learn what I truly am in the inner world and to unlearn what I truly am not in the outer world.

Finally, it is never too late for me not only to have a heart-to-heart talk with my Inner Pilot, but also to grow into His very image. I know that my Lord Supreme will be pleased with me totally only when I become like Him, another God, for what He wants from me is an equal share. He wants me to be His compatriot and not His slave.

Yes, there is one thing which it is too late for, and because I am too late for that, I am infinitely grateful to my Beloved Supreme. And what is that thing? It is my desire-life. It is too late for me to go back to my desire-life. Something more which is also true: I shall never be able to go back to the animal kingdom, never!

EA 82. 20 *July 1977, 6:15 a.m. — Jamaica High School Track, Jamaica, New York.*

83. GOD HAS MADE THIS WORLD ROUND

God has made this world round. Do you know why? Perhaps you do know. As a matter of fact, everybody will be able to supply an answer according to his and her inner light and outer perspective. According to my inner awareness, I wish to say that God has made this world round so that we all can sit around Him in a circle, and nobody's view will be obstructed by others. If some people obstruct our view, then naturally we shall feel sad and miserable. Therefore, God, the Author of all Good, has made our world round so that we can see Him easily and directly; and if we want to, which we should, we must look at Him devotedly and soulfully.

In order to be a member of God's ring, we have to remain inside our hearts. How do we remain inside our hearts? There are many ways, but the easiest and most effective way is to feel that the ring that God has created for us is not only our saviour-ring but also our brother-ring and sister-ring. If we consider the ring, the round world of ours, as a foreign element or an obstruction and barrier, if we feel that we have to go beyond the ring and, in order to do so, break asunder the ring, then we shall be committing an Himalayan blunder. No, that ring is our oneness-ring from where we can see our Beloved Supreme all at once, according to our heart's receptivity and our soul's luminosity and our life's selfless creativity.

EA 83. *20 July 1977, 6:20 a.m. — Jamaica High School Track, Jamaica, New York.*

84. AM I A GIVER?

Am I a giver? Yes I am. Am I a cheerful and soulful giver? No, unfortunately I am not. That means I am offering not only my rose but also many, many thorns along with it.

Am I a giver? Yes I am. Am I a cheerful and soulful giver? No, unfortunately I am not. That means I am offering not only my hope-world but also my frustration-world along with it.

Am I a giver? Yes I am. Am I a cheerful and soulful giver? No, unfortunately I am not. That means I am offering not only my aspiration-free world but also my desire-bound world to all those who are around me.

How can I become a cheerful and soulful giver in order to liberate myself and liberate others? I can become a cheerful and soulful giver provided I can feel that a giver is he who is also a receiver. The greater a giver he is, the better a receiver he becomes. He gives because he feels that that is the only way to please the real in him, the soul. The real giver gives to the world his soul's all-illumining beauty cheerfully and soulfully, and never, never does he give his body's ugliness-dream.

EA 84. 20 *July 1977, 6:35 a.m. — Jamaica High School Track, Jamaica, New York.*

85. IS IT MY FATE?

"My Lord Supreme, is it my fate that I shall have no short-cut to my satisfaction-goal? Everybody knows that there is a short-cut to the goal, but in my case I have not yet discovered that short-cut. You want me to love the world, You want me to serve the world because inside the world is Your own Reality-existence. But this world of Yours was not ready, is not ready and perhaps will never be ready for any chosen instruments, supremely chosen instruments, to awaken the slumbering human life. No! No spiritual figure has ever succeeded according to Your inner Volition. Perhaps You expected, expect and will always expect more than the sleeping world can offer to You, to Your direct emissaries. My Lord Supreme, do tell me what was the main obstacle and what is the main obstacle for my brother-sister friends who came into the earth arena to change the face of the world radically as I am also trying to do?"

"Only one obstacle you have, only one obstacle they had, and this obstacle is, and has always been, insurmountable. Do you know what that obstacle is? Disobedience, which grows into world-defiance. The seed of this disobedience is lack of oneness-heart. My son, unfortunately there is no short-cut for you, for you have become inseparably one with Me. God-realised souls have no short-cuts, for they have accepted My burden as their own burden. This world denies and defies all short-cuts, but you and I and others who are in the same boat have to make friends with our Eternity's patience."

EA 85. 20 *July 1977, 6:45 a.m. — Jamaica High School Track, Jamaica, New York.*

86. WHAT AM I DOING?

What am I doing? Am I loving God the man? No. Am I serving man the God? No.

What am I doing? Am I crying for a better world? No. Am I thinking of transforming my outer life? No. Am I contemplating fulfilling my inner life? No.

What am I doing? Am I desiring a world-destruction? No. Am I desiring to start a new life, so I can play once more like a child — carefree, with no mind, no thought, no doubt, no suspicion, no fear, no anxiety? Those golden days of my childhood am I longing for? No, no.

What am I doing? Am I showing my excessive attachment for Heavenly bliss, for the cosmic gods and goddesses? No, no. Am I showing a bitter, disgusted repulsion for the world, for this uncomely, unaspiring world? No, no.

What am I doing, then? I am just sailing my hope-boat towards a shore. Perhaps it is an uncertainty-shore and perhaps it is a dream-blossomed shore; but I do not know and I do not want to know, either. If I know that it is an uncertainty-shore, then I shall be doomed to destruction-frustration, and if I know that it is a dream-blossomed shore, then shameless complacency-relaxation will percolate through my entire being and dominate my earthly existence. Therefore, I leave my fate entirely at the Feet of my fate-maker, my Beloved Supreme.

EA 86. *20 July 1977, 8:10 a.m. — Jamaica High School Track, Jamaica, New York.*

87. WITHOUT MAN AND WITHOUT GOD

Without man can I do anything? Yes, I can. Without man I can do many, many, many things, if not each and every thing. If I pray to God to grant me the capacity to do everything without man's help, humanity's help, I am sure He will grant me the boon.

Without man I do so many things precisely because my Almighty Father, My Beloved Supreme, has given me the capacity. I look at my powerful brother, the sun, without man. I look at my beautiful sister, the moon, without man. I look at my sweet children, the stars, without man. I look and look at my Father, God, without man. I look at my Mother, God, without man.

But can I do anything without God? No, impossible! Why? I cannot do anything without God because I cannot live without God. How is it that I cannot live without God? Is it because He is all Kindness, all Love? No, no! Is it because He is all Concern, all Compassion? No, no! Is it because He is all-where? No, no! Is it because He is my essence and my substance? No, no!

Then why is it that I cannot live without God? I cannot live without God precisely because I cannot live without that which I have and that which I am. Can you live without what you have and what you are? Impossible! If you have light, you live in light and you are that light Itself. And if you have God within you, then you not only possess God but you are that very God. It is like a deer that has fragrance, musk. When the deer develops musk, the deer and the musk are inseparable. When the flower has fragrance, the flower and the fragrance are inseparable. Similarly, God the Beauty that is within me and God the possessor of the Beauty are inseparable. Therefore, I cannot live without God, for He is what I am and what I have. You too cannot live without what you have and what you are. What you have and what you are will always be the same Reality-Existence: God. Therefore, you and I cannot live without God, not to speak of doing anything without God.

EA 87. 20 *July 1977, 8:15 a.m. — Jamaica High School Track, Jamaica, New York.*

88. MY HEART-TO-HEART TALK

"O man, let Me have a heart-to-heart talk with you. Man, I love you and I serve you. But you do not believe in My Love, you do not believe in My Service. To My sorrow you suspect Me. To My sorrow you feel that My Love is binding you, binding you to the earth-bound reality. You feel that My Love has enchained you, entangled you, encaged you. You want to be a free bird, a free reality-existence, but you feel that My Love for you is binding you in every possible way. This is the realisation you have come to, man.

"I am having a heart-to-heart talk with you, so I wish to tell you that in no way am I binding you. I am only helping you, with My Love and with My Service, to become one with Vastness, one with Immensity, one with God's Eternity, Infinity and Immortality, one with Oneness-Delight itself. This heart-to-heart talk of Mine, man, one day you will believe. One day you will have faith in My soulful Message, My Life's breathless Message, that I have just offered to you."

"O Lord, let me have a heart-to-heart talk with you. O Lord Supreme, I do not love You, I do not serve You, in spite of the fact that at times I am fully determined to love You and serve You conditionally, even if it is not within my capacity to love You unconditionally. But alas, I fail to love You even conditionally; I fail to serve You even conditionally. My Lord Supreme, is it because I love mankind more than I love You? Is that why real love does not come from me towards You? Is it because You are not to be loved the way I want to love You, with all my earthly needs and Heavenly needs, with all that I think of as my needs? Is it because I am self-sufficient without You? To be without man is not an impossibility; but to be without You is impossibility itself. But is it because to some extent I can live without You? When I live in my ignorance-night, I do not live in You or for You. Or is it because my pride, my disproportionate pride, finds it beneath its dignity to live with You inside mankind? Is it because of all this that I am separated from You and find it impossible to offer true love to You? My Lord, will I ever be able to love You devotedly, will I ever be able to serve You soulfully, will I ever be able to claim You as my own, very own, founded on the inner conviction that You are mine and I am Yours? Will I ever be able to serve You and love You to my heart's content?"

"My child, what do you want? Do you want to love Me or do you want to prove to Me that you love Me? There is a great difference between your love for Me and your demonstration of love. Your love of Me and your wish to demonstrate your love for Me are two different things. You do not have to demonstrate your love to Me as long as you have the inner cry to love Me. This inner cry is not theoretical, but practicality itself. It is the height of practicality. I am the eternal Lover and you are My mirror, so you have to know that when I look at you I see My own reflection. Remain My mirror and My Love of you will be your love for Me, for I see Myself alone here on earth and there in Heaven. I do not see anything as something other than Myself. I do not see anybody as someone else. I see only Myself, My larger Self, My universal Self, through you, My mirror. Through you I see Myself, My own reflection. Therefore, you do not have to prove your love for Me. Just maintain your inner cry to love Me devotedly, soulfully and unconditionally. This inner cry is not only My divine Will in you, but it is also My supreme execution of My divine Will in and through you. I love My creation. Therefore, I live in My creation. If it just cries to love Me, that is more than enough. I need no other proof. That is proof itself: the cry, the cry, the soulful cry, only for Me, only for Me."

EA 88. 20 *July 1977, 8:20 a.m. — Jamaica High School Track, Jamaica, New York.*

89. NEVER MAKE AN OUTER PROMISE

My brother Chitta used to tell me, "Never, never make an outer promise. Only promise to yourself inwardly what you want to do in your life and with others' lives. The moment you outwardly tell the world what you are going to do, or what you expect others to do for you, for others, or for themselves, the hostile forces will invariably attack you directly. Then other undivine forces will try to enter into you: humanity's jealousy, humanity's insecurity, humanity's doubt and many wrong forces.

"When your promise is in the inner world, the undivine forces remain dormant. They think that it is just wishful thinking. When you are talking to yourself inwardly, they think it is not really a promise. But when you open your mouth for the public to hear, for humanity to hear, then you are exposed. At every moment your inner will has to come forward to fulfil your promise; otherwise, if you are unable to fulfil your promise, you will be assailed by self-doubt and self-mockery. The world does not have to mock at you. You yourself, your own sincerity, will mock at you. So it is better to keep your promise inside your heart: not to deliver it from your tongue and not to keep it even on the tip of your tongue."

Here I am not listening to my brother; I am not doing the right thing. All the time I am making outer promises: I will write so many songs, I will paint so many pictures, I will do this, that. But in my case, I am a spoilt child in the family. I do exactly the opposite of what they ask me to do. Therefore, I am paying the penalty very nicely with my disciples. And I am not only the spoilt child in my family, I not only exploited my family's affection and love, but I also exploit the Love,

Affection, Blessing and Compassion of my Beloved Supreme every day, every hour, every minute, every second. I always feel that if something comes out of my mouth, then He will be there to keep my promise, justify my promise. This is my inner conviction. I know I was nothing, I am nothing, I will remain nothing in humanity's eye. But in my Father's Eye, in my Father's Heart, I am everything, for I love Him, I need Him only, only, only.

EA 89. 20 *July 1977, 8:30 a.m. — Jamaica High School, Jamaica, New York.*

90. STRUGGLE

"My Lord Supreme, do You approve of my struggle-life? Do You approve of the progress that I make through struggle? I feel that I make progress only when I have struggles; only when I have to surmount obstacles do I feel that I make progress."

"My child, you are totally mistaken. The spiritual life, the real life, does not need struggle at all. There are two kinds of struggles that originate either from inside your existence or from outside your existence. Inside you are fear, doubt, anxiety, worry, suspicion, insecurity, impurity and many wrong forces. These wrong forces at times run riot. Again, these wrong forces are also to be found outside your body-reality, outside your own existence-reality, and they come to attack you. When you bring to the fore your own wrong forces, when these forces from within come to the fore, your struggle starts. Again, when the forces from outside attack you, your struggle starts. So what you have to do is to illumine the wrong forces that are within you so that they can become positive forces. And the forces that are attacking you from outside have to be challenged, fought and conquered.

"You are saying that you make progress only when you have struggles to face. You may think that the life of struggle is an opportunity to make progress. But there may be some other factors which you do not at all see. A life of struggle can easily become a life of revolt. You struggle to receive something, to fulfil your desire; but there comes a time when you see that there is no hope of fulfilling your desire-life. Then you just give up because you are frustrated, and from frustration comes revolt. You pray so hard, you meditate so hard, you do so many things to please Me, but because I do not fulfil your desire, you feel that I am not pleased. Then what do you do? You give up. Something more you do. You become frustrated and you may revolt against My Existence. Then you will stop praying and meditating and not try to keep consciously any connection with Me."

So I always tell the disciples to be careful. A life of struggle does not indicate a life of progress. There are many forces around you, many obstacles around you, which are unwanted and uncalled for. So do not bring to the fore your own wrong forces, which take the form of struggle. No, no, that is the wrong way. Do not add more unlit forces and create more problems for yourself. No, no, just have a childlike attitude. Be spontaneous, be happy. A child does not create problems so that he can get a smile from his parents. He is spontaneously doing everything, and from his spontaneous action he is making his parents happy. The Creator and the creation are also like that. When the creation offers a smile to the Creator, at that time the Creator is immediately fed and nourished. He feels that He has got everything.

When the child smiles, even if it is just a tiny smile, the mother feels that she has got the entire world. Similarly, when the mother smiles or the father smiles, the child feels that he has got the entire world. The mother is a beggar and the child is also a beggar. Here also, God the Creator and God the creation are equally beggars. Or you can say that they can become complete, integral and whole only when they exchange their mutual smiles.

As seekers you have to offer your smile through spontaneous action, for spontaneous action itself is the smile. So only grow in that smile. Act like a child: be spontaneous in everything that you do and say. Inside that spontaneity you will see your smile, and inside the smile you will see your spontaneity. Your smile and God's Smile are keeping each other alive. And they will do so throughout Eternity. What God and men need from each other is a soulful smile, a fruitful smile. Inside that tiny seed of a smile the entire cosmic Life-Tree exists. So do not try to build your life through struggle. That is the wrong way. Do not follow the way of struggle: follow only the way of spontaneity, the way of spontaneous smile, which is the only nourishment, the only fulfilment for God and man.

EA 90. *20 July 1977, 12:15 p.m. — Sri Chinmoy Centre, Jamaica, New York.*

91. SPECIAL MESSAGES

Our Beloved Lord Supreme has a special message for you today. He will grant you and your mind, peace. From today you will have peace of mind.

Our Beloved Supreme has a special message for him. Today, our Beloved Supreme will grant him and his heart love. His heart will be inundated with love.

Our Beloved Supreme has a special message for me. He will grant me and my life a continuous flow of assurance: that I am of Him and I am for Him.

Do you have any special message for our Beloved Supreme? Does he have any special message for our Beloved Supreme? Do I have any special message for our Beloved Supreme?

Do you have any special message for the Supreme? Your silence tells me that you do not have any special message for the Supreme, but I wish to tell you that you do have a special message. You means your soul; your soul is now speaking through me. The message that your soul, the real in you, has for the Supreme is this: "From now on, you will sail in His Boat cheerfully and unreservedly."

Does he have a special message for the Supreme today? His silence indicates that he has no special message for the Supreme today, but I wish to tell him that he does have a special message although he is not aware of it. His soul, which is the real in him, has a special message for the Supreme, and this message of his soul I am executing through his outer mind. The special message that he and his soul have for the Supreme is this: "From now on he will become consciously, soulfully and unconditionally a pure and sure instrument of the Beloved Supreme." This is his promise to our Beloved Supreme.

Do I have a special message for the Supreme? I do have a special message for the Supreme; I am fully aware of my own special message: "I want to live only for Him. When death is necessary, I want to die only for Him. But I know in the inmost recesses of my heart that my Lord is Infinity's Life, Immortality's Life, Eternity's Life. If I fulfil Him in His own Way, then I will enter into the infinite, eternal, immortal Life. Then there can be no death for me, no death in my sight." This is the special message that I want to offer to my Beloved Supreme: that I live only for Him and I shall die only for Him.

Each special message is the harbinger of the new dawn, a new revelation, a new fulfilment. Each special message is nothing short of a soulful and fruitful message. Each message begins a new life of self-recovery from the ignorance-world. Each new message is a self-discovery in the world of self-awareness. Each new message is a process of self-offering which eventually excels and transcends our highest imagination; each new message is our transformation into God's very image.

We are pleased with God when God offers us a special message. In God's case, He is not only pleased with us when we offer Him a special message, but also He is proud of us for He feels that our message is not only a message but also a promise. It is not only a promise but also the harbinger of a new dawn. It is not only the harbinger of a new dawn but also an all-fulfilling satisfaction.

EA 91. 20 *July 1977, 12:30 p.m. — Sri Chinmoy Centre, Jamaica, New York.*

92. TRANSFORMATION

Transformation is a house. It becomes a home only when there is peace, joy, harmony and love. Before that, the house is there — an amalgam of bricks, sand, wood and other material objects; but these things are useless and meaningless unless there is peace, love, joy and oneness inside the house. When these qualities or these capacities are visible, then the house becomes a home.

Human life is totally meaningless unless there is love in it. It is a life, a creation of God, but this creation of God is of no avail unless and until there is love in it. When love fills life, then only life is meaningful and fruitful. The transformation of house into home is what we need, the transformation of life into love is what we need.

The human mind we consider as the highest achievement on earth. But this mind is of no avail unless and until vastness becomes its other name. Unless and until the mind becomes synonymous with vastness, the mind is of no use. The mind always tries to maintain its superiority. It finds faults with others and suspects others. It gets pleasure only in exercising its individuality. Who needs that mind? But when vastness enters into the mind, the mind is illumined and fulfilled.

The creation as such we do not need, for it is helpless, hopeless, useless. But when we see God inside the creation, what we see is not helplessness but hope. What we see is not uselessness but usefulness. What we see is not mere promise but a faultless assurance of the fulfilment of that promise. So inside the creation, if we can see the Creator, then only is the creation meaningful and fruitful. Otherwise, earthly creation is of no avail.

A life of aspiration, a life of dedication, a life of concentration, meditation and contemplation cannot lead us far, very far unless it can make us feel that we came into the world only to please God and serve God in His own Way. Otherwise, we will have aspiration, we will have dedication, we will have concentration-power, meditation-power and contemplation-power, and these things will undoubtedly take us to a destination. But this destination need not be and cannot be the real destination which our God has kept for us. Inside each prayer, inside each concentration, meditation and contemplation there has to be a remembrance of our promise to God, that Him to please in His own Way we came into the world. Each time we pray, each time we meditate, each time we contemplate, each time we do anything, if there is no remembrance of our promise to God and if there is no self-assurance that we can keep this promise, then it is useless. No matter how many hours we pray, no matter how many hours we concentrate and meditate, everything will eventually end in bitter frustration. The results we shall get without fail from our prayer, concentration, meditation and contemplation, but these results will be far from our satisfaction.

We have set up a goal according to our own inner perception, and this goal we will reach. But just because we have set our goal according to our own inner image, we will not be satisfied; we will be frustrated. But at every moment when we pray, when we concentrate, when we meditate, when we contemplate, if we can keep in the forefront our soulful promise to our Beloved Supreme, and if we can keep our inner assurance, then we can and will fulfil this promise — that Him to please in His own Way, we saw the light of day. Then only will our prayer, concentration, meditation and contemplation have true value, true meaning, true fulfilment. Life has to become love. Mind has to become vastness. Creation has to become God. Prayer and meditation have to embody self-assurance and remembrance of our promise to God. Then only satisfaction, complete satisfaction, everlasting satisfaction, will dawn.

EA 92. 20 *July 1977, 12:40 p.m. — Sri Chinmoy Centre, Jamaica, New York.*

93. WHY DO I NOT SHARE?

Do I share my inspiration with you? No. Do I share my aspiration with you? No. Do I share my dedication with you? No. Do I share my experiences with you? No. Why do I not share my inspiration, aspiration, dedication and experiences with you? The reason is very simple. I feel that if I share these things with you, then I shall not remain unique. You will have the same things that I have, and my supremacy will go away. Even if you get the things that I have in a tiny, small measure, you will be able to claim that you, too, have the same as I. Then it is only a matter of time before you get the same amount as I have or far surpass me. So I am afraid of you. I am insecure, and I become jealous of you. Therefore, I do not want to share with you. My satisfaction will come to an end the moment I share anything with you, for then you and I will be on the same footing, which I don't want. I want to be at least an inch above you so that I can lord it over you. Alas, alas, this is the realisation I have come to.

When I dive deep within I see my eternal Friend, my only Friend, my Eternity's Friend, my Beloved Supreme. I see Him all the time sharing with me, with the rest of the world, with His entire creation. His inspiration, His aspiration, His dedication, His experience — everything that He has and everything that He is He shares with me and with all. Why? Why is He not afraid of losing His Supremacy, His Individuality, His Personality, His Lordship? If He grants me, grants us, what He has, if He grants even a portion of it, will it not make Him a lesser reality, will it not make Him incomplete?

My Lord Supreme tells me that I am a stark fool. When He gives me something, He does not lose. On the contrary, He increases. His offering of inspiration, aspiration, dedication and experience is like a flow of a river. When a river flows, meandering, it does not lose. Only it covers more territory, more land. His inspiration, aspiration, dedication, experience — everything that He has He carries with Him. He does not separate these things from His Existence. He carries, carries it all to us. From me it goes to you, from you it goes to somebody else. So His experiences, His achievements, His attributes, His possessions He never loses. On the contrary, He only distributes them here, there, elsewhere. He wants them to be spread all over, for He knows that the entire creation belongs to Him.

My uniqueness I want to show to the world with my sense of separativity. I exist for myself and I want to tell and show the world that I am one symbol, that nobody else is my carbon copy. At the same time, I do not want to be the carbon copy of anybody else. No, I want to be unique in my own way. Nobody will equal me, nobody will have the same shape, same pattern, same mould, same existence-reality as I have or I am. This is how I think of my uniqueness.

But my Lord Supreme has a different way of looking at His Uniqueness. He feels that His Uniqueness is expressed only when He sees His achievements and possessions here, there, everywhere. By making everyone His own, very own, by feeling that everyone is His and that He belongs to everyone, by feeling that He is for them and they are for Him, He feels His own Uniqueness in each. My uniqueness I want to establish with a sense of separativity. His Uniqueness He wants to establish with a sense of multiplicity. His entire

Vision-Light He wants to dedicate to His creation, for He feels that only the acceptance of His Light by the creation can make Him universally lovable, universally fulfilling and fulfilled. Therefore, he wants this kind of uniqueness: the One with the many, the One with all, a oneness-song with a oneness-reality. At every moment He wants oneness-creation. The Oneness-Creator wants to sing His oneness-song with His oneness-creation, for He feels that this is the only way His Uniqueness can be manifested throughout the length and the breadth of the world.

EA 93. *20 July 1977, 12:50 p.m. — Sri Chinmoy Centre, Jamaica, New York.*

94. SUBSTITUTES

We substitute quite often, but God does not need any substitute. When we play a game, if a member of our team is injured, immediately we get a substitute. For everything that we do on earth, we are apt to have a substitute, if necessity demands. But in God's case, He does not need a substitute. On His team, He never wants a substitute. Why, why?

God wants you to be on His team and occupy a special place, a special post. He wants you to be at a particular place, to do a particular thing in His cosmic Game. He wants you to play at a particular game at a particular place. You may say that today you are sick, today you are not in a cheerful frame of mind, today you are disturbed, today lethargy is disturbing you; you may have millions of reasons why you want to take rest and get a substitute.

But God will say, "You want a proper substitute, but do you not realise that each and everyone has been designated a post, a career. In My cosmic Game I want you to play a special game and occupy a special role. Now, if you want to offer Me a substitute, that particular substitute will be out of place: he will have his own part to play. If I ask you in the cosmic football game to play centre forward, and if I ask a friend of yours to play right wing, just because you are not in a cheerful frame of mind, just because you are disturbed, just because you are angry with Me, just because something is wrong with you, if you want somebody else to replace you, do you not think that that particular person will not have his own post? If he plays your part, then his part will not be executed by him or by anybody. If you constantly send in a substitute, if the whole world wants to send in substitutes, then how can all the parts, how can all the careers that have to be fulfilled in My creation be fulfilled?

"On My Cosmic team I shall never accept a substitute for you. You have to play your part, he has to play his part. If I take him away to play your part, his part will remain empty. No, everybody has to play his own part; then only we can fight against ignorance. If each one is at his proper place, if each one is playing untiringly, soulfully and unconditionally to please Me, then only can I fight against ignorance. Then only in the tug-of-war between the undivine and the divine, between ignorance-existence and wisdom-light, will we win. Never will I accept a substitute. To accept a substitute is to weaken the team. If we replace a particular player, then who is going to fill the place that remains empty?"

So there can be no substitutes on God's team. You play your role, let him play his role and let me play my role. Then only our Pilot Supreme, our Captain Supreme, is bound to win the victory. And this victory is for whom? Not only for Him, but for us as well; for we are one, eternally one. Father and children are eternally one, Mother and children are eternally one. So there can be no substitutes in God's Cosmic Game.

EA 94. 20 *July 1977, 1:00 p.m. — Sri Chinmoy Centre, Jamaica, New York.*

95. NOW

We are always apt to say that it is not too late to do anything, but do we ever say that it is not too early to do anything? It is not too early to do anything in life. It is not too early to pray in the small hours of the morning. It is not too early to realise God. It is not too early to reveal God. It is not too early to manifest God. The sooner we realise God, the sooner we reveal God, the sooner we manifest God, the sooner we will start with a new beginning, aiming at a higher, more illumining, more fulfilling goal.

In the spiritual life there is no such thing as early. This moment, the eternal Now, is the only saviour, only liberator, only fulfiller. To get up early in the morning, at three o'clock, to meditate is a difficult task. But if you say it is too early, then I will say you are mistaken. You are mistaken because what you call early or late is decided by your mind. It is the discovery of your mind that three o'clock is early, six o'clock is late. It is the mind that tells you three o'clock is too early, eight o'clock is too late. If you go beyond the mind, there is no such thing as an early hour or late hour. There is only one hour, that is God's Hour. And where is God's Hour? It is inside the Now. What is the Now? The Now is God the Preparation, God the Aspiration, God the Evolution and God the ever-transcending Perfection.

EA 95. 20 *July 1977, 1:15 p.m. — Sri Chinmoy Centre, Jamaica, New York.*

96. I KEPT PRAYING

Many, many years ago I started praying. One day God, my Beloved Supreme, came up to me and said, "I am satisfied with you, My son. I am granting you Peace."

I kept praying. A few years later He came to me and said, "I am pleased with you, My son. I am granting you Light."

I kept praying. A few years later my Lord Supreme came again. He said, "I am pleased with you, My son. I am giving you Delight, Nectar-Delight."

I kept praying and a few years later He came and said, "Son, I have given you Peace, I have given you Light, I have given you Delight. What more do you want? Is there anything else that you want? Is there anything else that you need? If one has Peace, Light and Delight, one has everything. Inside Peace, Light and Delight is world-power, world-satisfaction, world-oneness, world-fulfilment." I remained silent, and I kept on praying. My Lord left in silence, granting me a sweet little smile.

A few years later He came and said to me, "I see what you want. You want to become like Me, another God. Look, in the twinkling of an eye I am making you into another God. Are you satisfied?" I kept silent; I kept praying, praying.

He said, "I have made you like Me, another God. Even then you have to pray? What else do you need? Peace, Light, Delight, oneness, equality — everything I have given you. What more do you need? What more?" I remained silent. I kept praying.

My Lord said, "I know what you want. You want to play hide-and-seek with Me. You want to play the game of divine Lover and supreme Beloved with Me. This is what you want.

I grant you this boon." I gave my Lord a soulful smile and He granted me His all-loving, all-energising and all-fulfilling Embrace.

EA 96. 20 *July 1977, 1:30 p.m. — Sri Chinmoy Centre, Jamaica, New York.*

97. NEWNESS

Yesterday I saw you. Today I am seeing you for the second time. That means you are no longer new to me, no longer a stranger to me. You have become an old friend of mine; you and I have become old friends. Your age has increased and mine has too. You have aged and I also have aged.

Yesterday I saw something for the first time. Today I am seeing it for the second time. That means that thing has become old. Yesterday I felt something for the first time; today I am feeling the same thing. Yesterday I ate something; today I am eating the same thing. That means my food has become old. It is no longer a new experience.

Anything that I see for the second time, anything that I do for the second time, anything that I feel for the second time is automatically aged. Age has descended upon him or upon it.

Similarly that very thing, that very person, will feel the same about me — that I have become old. Is there anything that can never be old? Yes, there is something and that thing is my heart's inner cry. This inner cry is ever new. Every day it assumes a new prayer-form, a new concentration-form, a new meditation-form. Every day it achieves something new from God. You may say that every day you can pray, but how can your prayer or meditation be new? But I wish to say that it is not only possible and practical, but inevitable.

You may think Peace, Light, Bliss, Power and a few other attributes of God are enough for you. But I wish to say it is not true. God is infinite, and His attributes are infinite. So easily you can have an infinite variety of prayer, concentration and meditation. Each prayer can easily be new. Each concentration can easily be new. Each meditation can easily be new.

Prayer defies age. Concentration defies age. Meditation defies age. Our inner cry is the mother and father of our prayer, concentration and meditation. So let us make friends with this inner cry. Let our body, vital, mind and heart make friends with this inner cry. With inner cry our entire existence, outer and inner, will become an ever new existence-reality, an ever new, ever fulfilling Dream of God in and through us.

EA 97. *20 July 1977, 5:00 p.m. — Sri Chinmoy Centre, Jamaica, New York.*

98. WHY ARE YOU IN A HURRY?

Why are you in a hurry? Do you think that your aspiration-train, which is bound for satisfaction-goal, is leaving soon and that your body, vital, mind and heart are not ready, that only the soul is ready? Is that why you are in a tearing hurry?

Why are you in a hurry? Do you think that God's Hour already struck while you were fast asleep? Is that why are you sad, embarrassed and fearful? Is that why you are in a tearing hurry to pray and meditate and thus see the Face of God?

Why are you in a hurry? Do you think that your promise to God has not been fulfilled? Do you think that the time has passed and your promise remains unfulfilled? Do you feel sad and miserable that you are not a man of truth? Do you feel you are not a true devoted and soulful instrument of God? Is that why you are in a hurry to meditate, to dive within to do the needful sooner than at once?

Why are you in a hurry? Is it because you desperately need a fruitful smile from your Beloved Supreme in response to your soulful cry? This soulful smile can alone give your life its life-breath; your heart its nourishment-love; your mind its nourishment-clarity; your vital its nourishment-integrity; and your body its nourishment-purity. Is it because of this that you are in a hurry?

If all these questions are answered in the affirmative, then I wish to say that you have every reason to be in a hurry. If today you miss your aspiration-train that is bound for realisation-goal, then rest assured you will have to wait indefinitely. So if you are on time, if you catch the aspiration-train that is heading towards realisation-goal, then you are bound to see everything that you wanted to see, feel everything that you wanted to feel and become everything that you wanted to become. So do not miss the aspiration-train.

EA 98. 20 *July 1977, 5:10 p.m. — Sri Chinmoy Centre, Jamaica, New York.*

99. DREAMING AND PLANNING

Are you sleeping? Then sleep. Are you dreaming? Then wake up. Are you planning? Then look up, look around.

If you are sleeping, then sleep; I have nothing to do with you. If you are dreaming, then I must say that I do have something to do with you. If you are planning, then I have everything to do with you.

He who is sleeping does not know what he has and what he is. But you are not sleeping; you are dreaming and planning. So you know what you have and what you are. Again, you have to know that your way of dreaming and my way of dreaming, your way of planning, and my way of planning, are different.

When you dream, you enter into a world which is constantly shaping and moulding a new world. You enter into the planning world, where you want to see the beginning, middle and end of your creative process. But if you become a genuine seeker, you will see that the creator in you and the preserver in you will never meet with an end. There is no end to their creation and preservation. Only they will meet with an ever-transcending reality.

Although your way of dreaming and planning and my way of dreaming and planning are not the same, still you have something and I have something. Your thing is not efficient. It is not effective. It is not perfect. But mine is efficient, effective and perfect. Therefore, I requested you or commanded you to wake up, to look up and look around.

If you have a hand, then you can think of somebody else also having a hand, although your hand may not be as powerful as his hand. If you have an eye, then you can feel that somebody else also has an eye. But your eye may not be as beautiful or as blessed with vision as his eye. If you have finite awareness, finite achievement, then you can be aware of the infinite possibilities of somebody else.

As a genuine seeker, you can know that your dream state is only the precursor of the reality state which somebody else has; you can know that your planning state is only the beginning or the precursor of a state that is far beyond what your mind can see, feel and achieve.

But you have something; therefore, you are bound to be given more. If you have nothing, then you will be given nothing. If you have a little bit of life energy, the doctor will inject the medicine. But if you are totally gone, the doctor is not going to give you any medicine. If you have a little hope, or if the doctor has a little hope in you and for you, then the doctor will apply medicine.

In your life's journey, if you have an iota of aspiration, then only God will give you infinite aspiration. You are trying to realise God with your planning mind, in your own way. So God says, "Poor fellow, he is at least trying. Let Me show him the right way, the most effective way." At that time, God shows you His Plan, but unlike the planning you do with your human mind, He shows His ever-transcending Vision.

When you give to God your way of doing something, God offers you His Way of doing that very thing. A child gives to the father a penny or nickel that he finds on the street. That is his only achievement, his only possession, and he gives it to the father. The child could have kept it hidden and used it to buy a piece of candy, but he gave his entire possession to his beloved father. The father feels that the child's treasure is infinitely more valuable than millions of dollars. Then he gives the child a five dollar bill.

If you can give your own human dreams unreservedly to the Supreme, then you will get His Reality-world. If you give for the sake of your own joy, your Father's Oneness-Heart with you will always grant you infinitely more than you need and deserve. For His Satisfaction lies only in giving, in making you His Eternity's friend, co-sharer, partner and compeer of His Infinity's Light and Immortality's Delight. So if you give what you have in your dream-world, He will give His Reality-world. If you give what you have in your mental-planning world, He will give you His direct Vision-world. He will give immediately His direct Vision-world, which will blossom into Perfection and Satisfaction-world.

EA 99. *20 July 1977, 5:20 p.m. — Sri Chinmoy Centre, Jamaica, New York.*

100. ARE YOU THE LAMP OF GOD?

"Are you the Lamp of God the Supreme?"

"Yes, I am."

"What do you do?"

"I lovingly kindle the flame of aspiration in the desire-world."

"Are you the Lamp of God the Supreme?"

"Yes, I am."

"What do you do?"

"I devotedly illumine the dedication-world."

"Are you the Lamp of God the Supreme?"

"Yes, I am."

"What do you do?"

"I soulfully feed God's salvation-world early in the morning. I unreservedly feed God's liberation-world in the afternoon. I unconditionally feed God's Realisation-world in the evening. Finally, I dine with my Satisfaction-Perfection Father, Friend, my All, at night."

"My Eternity's friend, you do so much for your Beloved Supreme, God the Supreme. Now I wish to do something for you. I shall collect the richest harvest of gratitude for you here on earth. I shall collect the richest harvest of pride for you, there in Heaven."

EA 100. *20 July 1977, 9:40 p.m. — Greenwich Public Library, Greenwich, Connecticut.*

APPENDIX

EDITOR'S PREFACE TO FIRST EDITION

During the first twenty days of July 1977, Sri Chinmoy delivered one hundred short talks. These talks were given at his public *esraj* performances, at picnics, even at a local high school playground after morning sports practice.

In very few ways, though, can these pieces really be called talks. They contain a rhythmic, almost musical quality more like blank verse than prose. More important, they express a flow of ideas so subtle and melodic that they cry out to be felt and assimilated on an intuitive plane. Before speaking, Sri Chinmoy would enter into a high meditative state and then speak extemporaneously.

These talks, then, are expressions of a state of consciousness far beyond the mind's reach: short, illumining bursts of light from the Master's boundless Realisation-Sun.

BIBLIOGRAPHY

EVEREST-ASPIRATION (4 VOLUMES)

SRI CHINMOY:

–*Everest-Aspiration, part 1*, New York, Agni Press, 1977.
–*Everest-Aspiration, part 2*, New York, Agni Press, 1977.
–*Everest-Aspiration, part 3*, New York, Agni Press, 1977.
–*Everest-Aspiration, part 4*, New York, Agni Press, 1977.

Suggested citation key is EA.

TABLE OF CONTENTS

Composition typographique par imprimerie
Ab Academia Aoidon, Paris & Lyon.

Un grand merci à Prof Knuth pour
l'utilisation avancée de TEX.

A LYON, LE 13 AOÛT LXXXVII Æ.G.

CPSIA information can be obtained
at www.ICGtesting.com
Printed in the USA
BVHW03*0705090818
523439BV00001B/2/P

9 781911 319139